DOG SHOW JUDGING

JUDGING

The Good, the Bad, and the Ugly

Chris Walkowicz

D1564241

Publishing

Wenatchee, Washington U.S.A.

Dog Show Judging
The Good, the Bad, and the Ugly
Chris Walkowicz

Dogwise Publishing
A Division of Direct Book Service, Inc.
403 South Mission Street, Wenatchee, Washington 98801
1-509-663-9115, 1-800-776-2665
www.dogwisepublishing.com / info@dogwisepublishing.com

Illustrations: Mary Jung
Graphic Design: Lindsay Peternell

ISBN: 978-1-929242-66-5

Printed in the U.S.A.

Praise for
Dog Show Judging

It covers all aspect of judging and delves into the actual mechanics of running your ring, and outlines the many problems that can occur. It also establishes the need for you to become comfortable in dealing with both dogs and people. It gives examples of errors that judges have made and how to avoid them. All of the necessary facts are collected at your fingertips and can save you a lot of research and many hours of tedious work.
Dorothy MacDonald, AKC Judge and *Gazette* columnist

Every dog show person from the totally novice exhibitor to the all-rounder will love this new book from the "Bearded Lady" Chris Walkowicz! Her good common sense approach to the realities of advancing as an AKC judge, and the mechanics of judging, is right on target. Exhibitors will love the insights into the judge's thoughts that Chris shares. And everyone will love the war stories that make judging of dog shows overseas like nothing else in the world. Pure fun on every level. This book will be a great asset for the dog world for years to come!
Steve Gladstone, AKC Exhibitor and Judge

To my Grandchildren
Lauryn, Michael and Calé Anne,
who fill my life and heart with joy.

And a lifetime of Grand Dogs
Justin, Caprice, Calli, Brandy, Favour, Kodiak, Katie,
Cody, Marcy, Sally, Bubbles, Tigger, ALF, Tootsie,
Bonny and Whoopi!

ACKNOWLEDGMENTS

Appreciation is given to fellow judges Sulie Greendale-Paveza and Linda Robey, as well as to fellow writers, Judie Gulley and Barb Foster, for their suggestions. And to all the judges who related their experiences!

To Mary Jung, who captures my every thought.

Thanks to my very patient editor, Larry Woodward from Dogwise Publishing, who managed to organize me. And all at Dogwise for caring so much about dogs and dog people.

And, of course, my great husband, Ed, who gives me unflagging support.

TABLE OF CONTENTS

INTRODUCTION

All dog show judges were once exhibitors. Thus every judge shares a variety of feelings and experiences with the exhibitors who enter their ring. Whether you are a judge, a judge wannabe, or an exhibitor, you will likely be bombarded with a mixture of similar feelings each time you set foot in a ring. These often combine a jangle of nerves, pride, and anticipation for judge and exhibitor alike. Should we win or be complimented on our judging skill, we're instantly hooked and reinforced. If we don't, we wonder what we could have done better.

We have all owned dogs who have wrapped us around a paw, a dog we dream of posing on the Best in Show pedestal or lying beside us in a room full of ribbons and trophies. But few of us start out as instant winners. For those willing to put forth the effort, however, we can learn what it will take to move down the path leading from the dog show parking lot, to the grooming tent, to the Best in Show ring. Or from a fun match in some small town to judging at Westminster.

Understanding Each Other Better
One of my goals in writing this book—in addition to easing the way for new and prospective judges—is to help judges and exhibitors better understand and help each other. Since we share so much in common, we should be working together toward a common goal—finding a great dog. If we understand each other better, both judges and exhibitors will be more successful.

One of the themes of this book will be to go inside the mind of the judge, particularly as it relates to what they expect and want from an exhibitor. And then to switch roles and look at what an exhibitor expects and wants from a judge. Of course, every judge was once an exhibitor and has the advantage of that experience. When I began judging, for example, I noticed the distracting things handlers do—and realized I'd done most, if not all, of them myself. Having been there and done that, I try to be as understanding as I can be.

Given our goal of working better in the ring together, let's take a quick look at a few things that exhibitors need to be aware of from the judge's perspective:

- Be on time. Watch a couple prior classes to learn the pattern. When you know what to do, you'll be more at ease.

- Be ready to set up your dog immediately and to move her at the best pace. First impressions count.

- Is your dog trained? Judges will put up with a few puppy antics, but they expect an adult to be well behaved. Have someone videotape you at training class so you can avoid mistakes and show your dog at the right speed. It's nearly impossible to give an award to a dog who is lying on his back or who looks more like a horse thundering to the finish line over one who is trotting easily alongside his handler.

- Make sure your dog is clean, with nails clipped and teeth brushed. This is so easy—well, maybe not if you own a dog twice as big as you—but it's priority number one.

- Watch the judge and pay attention to the action in the ring, rather than chatting—time enough for that later while you show off your ribbons.

Conversely, exhibitors have the right to expect certain things from the judge. A judge should be fair, honest, patient with puppies, willing to help newcomers to the sport, and offer a friendly smile or encouraging word—in other words—a regular scout. And do this despite rain, cold, sleet, melting heat, and an aching back. If a judge can't make the show a pleasant experience, a long vacation filled with rest and recreation is the prescription.

Deciding to Be a Judge
What makes someone want to enter the show ring and judge dogs? Whatever the triggering event, at some point in time certain dog fanciers decide they would like to become a judge. Maybe because they think they can do a better job than the last judge they showed under! It took me a long time to decide whether I wanted to contend with unhappy exhibitors, battle the elements, and put up with all the travel hassles. Handlers can escape the torrid heat or freeze-your-toes cold to momentary comfort where they can strip off pantyhose or add another layer. The judge can't, at least until lunch break. And those horrid classes of five. Eeek! So for 28 years echoing Scarlett O'Hara, I said to myself, "I'll think about that tomorrow."

Whether the idea of judging comes and knocks you on the head or sneaks up on you over time, the preparations you have to go through to become a judge will, at the very least, make you a better exhibitor and breeder. So while this book is oriented principally to new and prospective judges, anyone showing dogs can benefit from the advice, tips, and war stories included in the following pages.

This book is not meant to be a technical treatise on the finer points of judging—anatomy, gait, or in-depth discussions of breed type. Those subjects are well covered in a number of other books and articles. I have chosen to focus on the things a new or prospective judge needs to learn that one probably cannot read about elsewhere—and have fun doing it. This book is designed to make the process of deciding whether or not to attempt to become a judge easier and to shed light on how to make the life of a judge more successful and enjoyable. It will also assist the exhibitor in understanding the process of judging with all its mental and physical challenges and in deciding if joining the ranks of judges is the right thing for you.

How this Book is Organized

The book is divided into three sections. The first focuses on what it takes to become a judge—what experience and education is required—and the American Kennel Club (AKC) application process. The second section is a look into the nuts and bolts of being a judge (both in and out of the ring), focusing on those aspects not usually covered elsewhere. The last part is the fun part—tips, for both judges and exhibitors, and war stories from judges who have traveled the world judging dogs. While many are lighthearted, all should help you better understand the mental and physical challenges of judging no matter what role you play in the world of dog shows.

Chapter 1

THE PROSPECTIVE JUDGE

We show people love dogs. That's a given. Likely, you are reading this with a furry friend lying beside you. Look honestly at the dog who sits at your feet gazing at you with adoration. He can't see your faults and loves you despite your human flaws. As a dog owner the same should be true for you as you gaze back at your dog—even if he doesn't quite touch the stars and you can indeed see his faults.

In contrast to your role as an owner, a judge is paid to evaluate a dog objectively. To do that, you need to never stop learning more about dogs and gaining as much experience in the dog show world as you can. Committing to an intensive educational process is the first key to becoming a successful judge.

Education and Experience

The AKC has a number of requirements relating to education and experience in order to become an approved judge. In fact, once you make the commitment to judging, you will find yourself involved in a life-long learning process. Of course, the AKC also requires that you have extensive experience in owning, breeding, and exhibiting dogs. You can find all the details on the AKC web site—on the home page, click on the downloadable forms link and then search for the Conformation link under Judges.

Based on what the AKC requires and my own experience, here are the things beyond being an experienced "dog person" that I recommend you focus on:

- Keeping good records.
- Read, read, read.
- Finding mentors.
- Becoming a ring steward.
- Attending seminars and workshops.
- Judging at matches, sweepstakes, and futurities.

Keeping Good Records

AKC judging applications, procedures, and requirements change as often as the Midwest weather. And although the application process for judges is a never-ending quest for the perfect method, one of the requirements will always be to *document your experience.* The best way to do that is to keep accurate records of your dog-related career. Even if you have not yet decided to apply, if there's the slightest chance that you or anyone in your household will ever apply to judge, keep records of everything you do related to dogs. This means more than the records you're required as a breeder to keep by the AKC such as keeping track of litters, individual dogs, breedings, and so on. You might even want to jot down your grandmother's shoe size, just to be safe—especially if she was involved in the world of dogs in any way.

Since documenting your dog-related experience is part of the application procedure, maintain detailed records relating to breeding, showing, judging matches, as well as club memberships, positions, and responsibilities. All will contribute to your resume and the documentation will be invaluable when applying. Years later, you don't want to think, "How many Goosendorfer Hounds *did* I go over that day?"

Keep track of how many shows you attend per year—and which ones, particularly regional specialties, Nationals, and major shows with large entries. Every registered dog you've owned should be listed, along with their numbers. Every litter must be recorded, of course, with numbers and registered names. The litter registration number may be all you need, but better to keep more records than to scramble for mislaid or long forgotten information. Record Champions you've owned and those you've finished for others if you've handled—professionally or as a friend. This will keep you from having to remember their names and registration numbers ten or fifteen years from now when you finally decide you'd like to apply to judge.

Most of us belong to dog clubs, and you should keep records of this in addition to all that was mentioned above. The more active you are in a club, the more positions you will be able to list on your application. Document duties such as stewarding, show chair, and holding an office as these indicate your dedication and experience over the years.

With computers, keeping these stats is easy once you get set up to do it. But don't go through the angst of a crashed hard drive; be sure to keep back ups on cds and/or flash drives—or whatever newfangled thing is available after this book goes to print!

Read, Read, Read

Since most dog people are thirsty for information on their hobby (obsession is perhaps a better word!), I may be preaching to the choir to urge you to educate yourself by reading whatever you can get your hands on. Take advantage of all the relevant books, magazines, and web sites that you can find. The better educated you are, the easier it will be to pass the requirements to become a judge and then to advance further in your new career.

There's only one small problem with this quest for information. Some friends tell me they need to build an extra room for all their dog books! My particular problem is magazines. For me, dog magazines are like zucchinis. Once you plant the seed, you'll have a bumper crop. When you're showing, you might not be able to afford all the great magazine subscriptions. But when you become a judge, they appear in your mailbox like bills, catalogs, and credit card applications. My husband and I guess how many of each will appear each day. I hold the written word in the highest esteem, so I pore over every magazine, storing up more canine knowledge. And I even look at the pictures, studying the profiles. Sometimes, however, when I'm busy, the stack threatens to tumble over. Once a month, I dutifully pack them up to haul them to my club building. I don't dare miss a meeting, as the duffle bag weighs about 30 pounds each month. Oh, and a psychiatric nurse friend takes them to the hospital ward. She says they calm the patients!

Finding a Mentor

The best tip at every stage in the dog fancy is to find a mentor—someone who can teach you the nuances of the breed you've chosen. The most helpful mentor is one who isn't kennel blind, one who can see and appreciate the good characteristics of dogs other than their own. Not only will a good mentor further your education, you will need to list one or more mentors on your application when you apply to become a judge, even if you have been involved in your breed for thirty-plus years! This can be awkward if you feel you "know it all," so prepare to take a big bite of humble pie. If you are eligible to judge more than one breed initially, you will need to find mentors for these breeds as well.

Meet with your mentor(s) at shows, club meetings, and social events. Sit with him or her ringside and study the breed in question. Visit kennels to learn more about breed type. Go over dogs together. Good dogs. Great dogs. Dozens of dogs. When going over or putting hands on dogs and discussing them, start out by praising something you particularly admire in the dog. Every dog has something wonderful about them—eye color, good feet, or temperament. When you can express something positive to a handler, they will be more likely to evaluate their own dog honestly. Keep in touch with your mentors and keep going back to them, seeking them out and continuing discussions over the years—your educational process should never stop!

One of the best times to meet with your mentor is when attending a show where you're not exhibiting. When exhibiting, most of us tend to be distracted, grooming and preparing our dogs and ourselves for the ring. And then there's the natural bias we have toward our own dogs, our "style," and our friends. Use these shows as an educational experience rather than simply a social event or even a competition. Make honest judgments of others' dogs and ask questions of a breed expert if you are puzzled over a judge's placement. Even if you don't agree, store the information in a brain cell somewhere. You may actually realize, at a later time, that the other person's opinion was right!

Stewarding
Stewarding is a great way to gain experience working with a judge in the ring. And dog clubs are always on the lookout for more ring stewards at the shows they sponsor. Not only does stewarding add to your knowledge of judging, it is a great way to indicate your dedication to the sport and help clubs. And of course, acting as a ring steward is a requirement when you apply to become a judge!

Stewarding helps one learn ring procedure and will be a valuable part of your education. Ask the judge about her preference concerning ring procedure as well as hospitality courtesies. Mark your steward's book during the judging process in case anyone questions a placement later.

You'll be able to watch the judge's methods from inside the ring and many judges are happy to answer procedural questions during a break. You might even learn from their mistakes. (Yes, we judges do occasionally make mistakes!)

Efficient stewards are worth good salaries (although pay is either non-existent or minimal). You'll just have to be satisfied with a smile, thanks, lunch, and what you've learned throughout the day. Just realize that being a good steward will prove invaluable not only to the judge you're assisting, but to your own career.

Belonging to one of the many ring stewards organizations can be particularly helpful as other members will give you tips and show you the routine. Once ribbon sorting, juggling armbands, classes, and keeping exhibitors happy are second nature, you'll have taken a big step toward learning ring procedure. The keeping everyone happy part is probably the most difficult thing to master, but it will help you down the road, believe me!

Attending Seminars, Workshops, and Other Educational Events

You will need to document for the AKC that you have attended relevant seminars and educational events. Take advantage of as many of these opportunities as possible. Seminars of all types are helpful to both new and experienced judges. They're listed in the *AKC Gazette,* as well as in breed publications, and on websites. Local clubs may host events, but sometimes are only announced on a word of mouth basis. Whatever or wherever they are, go and go often.

Anyone who intends to judge (and, in fact, anyone who shows!) should attend seminars on their own breed, but don't ignore other breeds. Even a Saluki breeder who learns something about Bulldogs will come away more knowledgeable. And, some day, that Saluki breeder turned judge, should he decide to complete the Hound group and go on to more breeds, might have a Bulldog in his first Best In Show judging assignment. So, while you should naturally focus on events related to the breed or breeds you want to judge, don't stop there. Is there a seminar you can attend on movement? Absolutely you should go! Breeding and whelping—you bet! Anatomy, Structure, AKC Judging Operations, Junior Showmanship, they are all good choices.

Attending seminars can require a significant commitment on your part. A seminar might run a couple of hours in an evening or stretch over an entire weekend. While clubs often sponsor these events, expect to pay a registration fee and recognize that these fees usually barely cover the club's expenses. Think of them as an education with no books to buy, no college sweatshirts, no room and board expenses, and no long cafeteria lines. What a deal!

Another way to further your education is to join local judges associations for seminars, camaraderie, and good advice. National judging organizations are well worth the dues for the invaluable experience, newsletters and, best of all, institutes they provide. These institutes typically offer several breeds at one time. Some present breeds in one group at a time. Others provide a mix of breeds from various groups. I found it valuable to sit in on breed seminars from groups other than the one I was working on because maybe—Some Sweet Day—I would be able to judge Best In Show, and it would be nice to know what made an Affenpinscher a good Affen! Even if you don't attend each seminar, you can use the time to take a break and discuss a breed in depth with a long time veteran breeder.

Judges' study groups at National Specialties are also valuable, usually consisting of a seminar, packets of educational materials, dogs to go over for hands-on examinations, a critique, and ringside mentoring. These furnish valuable in-depth information for the prospective judge and are well worth attending. You can often make connections with a veteran breeder to use as an on-going mentor for some new breed. At these events, the purchase of that sweatshirt might be a good move if the show is outdoors and in inclement weather.

Institutes cover several breeds and are held over three to five days. These are truly canine colleges held by AKC and the various national judging organizations—American Dog Show Judges, Dog Judges of America, and Senior Conformation Judges Association. Any number from half to a full group of dogs are covered. Basic institutes cover procedures and all the fundamentals. Definitely try to attend these to stuff your brain full of dogs, dogs, dogs. About the time you sense information overload, a social event is held, with food, laughter, sometimes dancing, and definitely talk—about dogs, of course!

As you study more and more breeds, you will quickly learn what the outstanding characteristics (good and bad) of the breed are. As a long-time judge once said, "We learn on our customers."

Judging at Matches, Sweepstakes, and Futurities

Judging at these types of events is one experience that will help in your application. Unlike dog shows, assignments for matches, sweepstakes and futurities may be solicited—prospective judges are allowed to spread the word about needing match and sweepstake assignments and this, of course, increases your visibility factor. Let others know you're interested in their breed and you might receive an invitation. Most clubs are open to anyone wanting to judge a match. Some specialty clubs give sweeps assignments only to breeders, but many are delighted to meet someone who would like to gain more experience with a breed.

Many of these types of events offer Best Puppy, Bred-by-Exhibitor, or Veteran competitions. These are helpful in providing experience, compliance, and knowledge. If you're offered a Toy Group at one of these shows and you're starting in Working, remember your distant goal of presiding at a Best In Show and say "Yes!" Learning about Pugs may help you understand Mastiffs better some day. Obviously no club will ask you to judge at any kind of event unless you are a well known expert in your breed—hence going through all the above educational hoops will pay off when it comes to this step.

To count toward your judging requirements, a match must be a sanctioned match, i.e., one approved by the AKC. Matches used to draw entries the size of some smaller dog shows today. Those were the good old days when many of us enjoyed an entire day watching all sorts of breeds, tailgating with others, and practicing our trade—whether it be handling, judging, or evaluating our breeding program—without the pressure of a show or traveling hundreds of miles. We'd take entire litters, round up a Shepherd handler to take in a Pomeranian, and have a Norfolk breeder judge them. It was a learning process for all concerned.

These days, however, matches are scarcer than New Guinea Singing Dogs. Now they are typically held after shows and everyone—club members, exhibitors, and pups—are tired. Or they are held on the same day as a nearby point show, and so the entries are fewer. Nevertheless, they're still a great training

ground for all and a boon for judging applicants. Judges have the opportunity to put their hands on and evaluate all sorts of breeds. Even though you may never want to judge Greater Norwegian Turnip Eaters, some day they might be added to a group you do. The experience to judge and learn at this level along with the chance to work with additional breeds will make you a better judge down the road. Never pass up an opportunity to learn. Even those who never plan to judge can learn a lot standing in the center of the ring!

Sweepstakes and futurities are usually held before regional or national specialties, and should you have a chance to judge one of these, grab it. Most likely, a number of quality entries will be present. These are good opportunities to determine whether you really have the interest in taking your dog show activities one step further into judging. They're also great training grounds for learning protocol and putting your evaluation skills to work. Then watch the regular point show which follows with a mentor by your side and compare. If the breed judge picks different dogs than you do, don't despair. You might learn to place a higher priority on certain characteristics. Or the dogs could be in different classes or misbehave. Vivá la difference! That's what makes a dog show and gives hope to all of us who don't win on a given day.

The Application Process

When you have completed the educational/experience requirements and have the required background in breeding and showing your breed, you are in a position to make a formal application to the AKC to become a judge. You should note that there are potential conflicts of interest that you need to be aware of that might disqualify you. For example, you or a close relative may have an occupation (your day job!) which might be deemed a conflict of interest such as working as a professional handler or selling dog food. To determine whether or not your day job as a toll collector or professor of music is one of those, check with the AKC's Judging Department by phone or on their website. If you meet those requirements, charge onward and upward.

If you haven't already done so, obtain a New Breed Judge application by writing or calling the AKC Judging Operations Department or by downloading one from the AKC website (www.akc.org). Make a copy and begin filling in the blanks as you complete the requirements. Make sure you have plenty of free time to unearth records and document your experience, especially if you have not been doing so all along. Don't do as I did, do as I wish I had. I had to dig through 30 years of boxes, drawers, and memories when I first applied to become a judge.

When you've completed all the requirements and filled in the application, take a copy of it to an AKC representative and ask him or her to review it. Then send it to the AKC Judging Operations Department where they will decide if you meet the requirements, i.e., deem you worthy! You'll then be scheduled for an interview, this is usually easy for your first breed—your breed of origin—since, of course, most applicants know them like a mother. It's also required that you pass a written breed test, an anatomy test, and a procedural exam. When you finish and return these, your name will be presented for consideration, and published in the *AKC Gazette* twice. This is not a speedy process, though faster than it once was. It's just like buying a new, supposedly speedy computer—it's still never fast enough! Plan to haunt your mailbox for approximately four to six months.

When the letter does appear granting you provisional status, wait (though not with "baited" breath) for the calls that invite you to judge at shows. Remember, unlike a match, you cannot solicit these invitations. It helps that the AKC gives clubs educational credit for inviting new provisional judges (those with one group or less). But the sad fact is there are approximately 3,200 judges and an average of only 20 to 30 all-breed shows each weekend. A hint—accept all the shows that invite you!

Provisional Status

Currently, the requirement for a provisional is to judge at five shows with entries—much easier for Lab, Sheltie, Golden, or German Shepherd judges than someone who's starting with American Water Spaniels or American Foxhounds. Some shows may not even have an entry in one of the less common breeds and you might have to wait months to get an assignment with an entry in your breed. On the other hand, in the past, provisional judges had to stop accepting assignments once they already had judged at five shows. Thankfully, this has changed, and you may accept as many shows as you want to help get you more experience. So count your blessings!

Regulations are in a constant state of flux, so be sure to keep up-to-date on any changes. Joining one, or all, of the above mentioned judges organizations and/or any local dog oriented group helps. This allows you to talk (or moan) to people with similar interests and who have trod the same path.

Keep track of your provisional assignments and entries on the form provided by AKC. Once you have judged the required number of shows and have been observed by reps, make a copy of the form and mail, fax, or e-mail it to the Judging Operations Department, with a request for approval of full status.

Then, assuming you want to be approved for additional breeds, you get to start all over again! If this is the case, it is wise to continue expanding your education on additional breeds while completing your provisional assignments. You will need to obtain an application for additional breeds by calling the Judging Operations Department or downloading it online. The requirements for additional breeds are different than those needed to obtain your original breed. These may (and likely will) change from time to time, but do focus on education as well as experience. If you aspire to become an all-breed judge, take your vitamins and pray you live long enough.

Keeping Visible

Visibility is a good way to obtain assignments. Judges are not allowed to solicit assignments, per AKC regulations, but show chairs are more likely to hire people they have met or heard good things about. So besides learning and enjoying yourself at dog shows, you'll have more contacts who may remember you for a judging slate in the future.

E-mail lists and online forums exist in abundance for breeds, show interests, and judges. Although keeping current takes time, sharing experiences helps keep your name in view. And you make many new friends without even traveling to see them! Definitely join sites of interest to judges. Even if you only lurk, you'll pick up many tips.

Be extremely careful, however, about perceptions. Yes, you can share your satisfaction in obtaining new provisional breeds with friends, but do not even hint you need assignments. Solicitations can cause a costly and lengthy suspension in your privileges.

Attend institutes and seminars where you'll meet other judges who are eager to learn and to share experiences. You might have a tale or two to relate yourself, and soon you'll have many new contacts and friends. Continue attending shows even if you're no longer exhibiting your own dogs. Volunteer to help a club. They're always looking for stewards, and by now your experience will be a real asset to the club. Introduce yourself to others. You'd be surprised at how many people are feeling new and hesitant themselves. It doesn't matter if they're newcomers, selling catalogs or scooping, these folks just might be a Show Chair or know one and recommend you. Show them your appreciation for their part in the show. They just might remember a friendly face and name to go with it. At the very least, you'll have a new acquaintance to chat with.

Chapter 2

NUTS AND BOLTS

But first.... "Whaaaat?" you think. Here I am packing my suitcase and practicing my photogenic smile.

One day, the phone rings—or you open your e-mail—and you have your first request to judge! You're ready to roll, feel confident about your ability to judge, and all of your credentials are in order. But before you commit to your first assignment, make sure you understand what I call the "nuts and bolts" of judging, the things you need to know that you are unlikely to learn reading Breed Standards or attending a seminar. These include:

- Contracts and communication
- Scheduling issues
- Travel considerations
- Being prepared…for anything!
- Money considerations
- Taxes
- Record Keeping

Contracts and Communication

A contract should arrive shortly after you have accepted an invitation to judge asking for your signature. You should also receive in writing—although not necessarily at the same time—a list of the breed(s) to which you have been assigned. The contract will lay out the applicable club requirements regarding fees and per diem expenses along with other instructions. Don't be surprised, however, if you have to contact a club for additional information, as some are better at communicating than others.

If you do not receive a contract within a month after you have accepted an invitation, contact the Show Chair (or Judges Committee chair) to determine when it will arrive. Should you receive another invitation in the interim which would involve a time conflict, you should tell the first club that you will wait only a specified amount of time or you'll accept the second invitation. With the internet so convenient, this gives you (and the club!) a speedy process with no need for procrastination on mailing. Realize, however, that local kennel club officers change (they are unpaid volunteers!) and paperwork can get lost, so mistakes do occur. Be sure to check the AKC or the show superintendent's website to ascertain you have been assigned the breed(s) specified in the contract.

Once you have received an invitation, if you have been approved for additional breeds, it is permissible for you to tell the club contact that you have new provisional breeds. For example, if you have recently gained provisional status for American Water Spaniels and have had difficulty getting an opportunity to judge them, by all means let the show chair know. It can be frustrating to have the assignment given to a veteran judge who has judged them for 50 years because the Show Chair did not know of your interest and availability.

Scheduling Issues

With your first assignment, you don't have to worry about scheduling conflicts (that will come later!). You just accept the invitation and mark off the days on your calendar. Once multiple invitations begin to come to you, however, it is much more important that you take care to note them on a calendar or other scheduling device. Calendars specifically geared toward the requirements of a judge have been developed. These cover several years, so when you receive an invitation for the next year, or the one after that, there is space to record it. I have included an example of the schedule spreadsheet I use on pages 30-33.

Be very careful you don't schedule conflicts inadvertently, although sooner or later we all seem to goof this up. AKC has certain restrictions they enforce about scheduling. You cannot accept judging assignments at locations within 200 miles of each other unless 30 days have passed. This means you can accept an assignment in New York City on January 3rd and another on January 10th in Miami—or you can accept one in Minneapolis on January 3rd and one in St. Paul on February 4th. In the second case, since the two locations are within 200 miles of each other, you have to wait at least 30 days between the two events. In any case, if you are contacted about judging at a show close to where you have recently judged, it is good etiquette to let the club know you have recently judged nearby even if it has been more than 30 days since this can reduce entries. Some clubs have additional time and/or mileage restrictions, so make sure you are aware of them. If you are unsure about distances, check with the website the AKC uses to determine mileage at www. indo.com/distance. If the show site changes or you do not have web access, call the AKC Judging Operations Department to make sure. The mileage restriction is as the crow flies, not based on driving on curvy roads.

Travel Considerations

You will not always be a hero in your hometown, so after the initial flurry of local people who invite you to judge within a drivable distance, accepting an invitation usually means flying the sometimes unfriendly skies. Learning how to be an efficient and prepared frequent flyer is a must for judges.

One of the first things you should do as a newbie judge, right after calling all your friends and telling them, no, you didn't win the lottery, but the next best thing—you've been accepted to judge!—is to obtain the right kind of credit card. Not just any credit card, but one that gives frequent flyer miles for every dollar you spend on travel and all other purchases. It's like having a fairy godmother. Shop and get credit—how much better could it get?

Unless you live in a major city and fly to a major city, flights are rarely nonstop. You might find yourself traveling from Westchester, New York to Atlanta to reach your hometown in Illinois. This usually means a full day of travel before and after shows due to layovers as you transfer flights. Layovers can be as short as 30 minutes, meaning you will have to run from one terminal to another with no time to grab a bite to eat...or the layovers are three hours, enough time for a sumptuous feast, but it always seems those three hours are not at lunch or dinner time, or the only food available is not on your diet!

When researching flights, I've found that the least expensive can usually be booked on late Tuesday night and Wednesdays. Staying over Saturday night helps bring down the price as well, something which you can usually take advantage of. New judges (and veterans, as well) often find it helpful to include an extra day in their plans, using the additional time to attend a specialty, to be mentored, or to visit a kennel to keep learning about more breeds.

Once the judging program arrives (or when you check online to see the schedule), you may find you could have booked an earlier flight home. Ask the Show Chair if the club would be willing to pay the difference to allow you to change flights so that you can leave earlier—many will agree if staying over would involve another night's motel and meal expenses.

Check out the discount travel sites on the internet to obtain a suitable schedule, even if you end up booking directly with the airline. I've saved myself 20 hour layovers by checking first! This works even if you use a travel agent. The benefit of using an agent is that person knows your preferences almost as well as you do. Crack-of-dawn flights or after work? Aisle or window? Red-eye to reach an Institute after a weekend of judging?

Then there are all the usual problems often associated with flying. If a suitcase is lost, report it immediately. Usually, the airline will deliver it to you within a few hours or a day at most. That is, unless you're in Podunkville, with nothing available but the Goodwill store, which has nothing in your size. Then it will take two or three days! Be prepared to iron.

Security is a necessary hassle, but a hassle nonetheless—sorting through liquids, taking off coats and shoes. Make sure you have allocated enough time to go through security. Now that most airlines are charging for luggage, make sure you budget for that if you are like me and always have a large suitcase (see next section). In some cases, having FedEx ship your luggage for you can make sense.

Generally, someone from the club will contact you before the show, asking for arrival plans, and giving motel and hospitality information. If you're of a particular age or don't want to haul bags up stairs, inquire whether the motel has an elevator or ask for a room near the lobby. In some cases, the club will pick you up at the airport, but check ahead so you will know if you will have to take a shuttle or rent a car instead.

Once you have arrived at the hotel, ask if a letter has been left for you if you have not already been informed about pick-up time to go to the show. Once in a great while, the club hasn't taken care of this important detail. Always have a phone number available of someone you can call in situations like this—the Show Chair, a club hospitality volunteer, or even another judge.

As a new judge, you may find you don't know many people. Walking alone into a restaurant in or near your hotel can be intimidating for some people. I always carry a book or magazine with me to occupy my time until my meal is served if I end up eating alone, but greeting anyone I know as I go by. Carrying Standards, a dog magazine, or the show schedule is a good way to identify yourself as a judge. Once recognized as a judge, you'll likely be invited to eat with other judges or club officials who are dining there. Most judges are friendly to others, remembering when they were in that newbie spotlight. The next morning, as all gather in the lobby, introduce yourself to anyone you don't know. These people will soon be your friends.

Some clubs host judges' dinners. These are fun if held early enough since most of us like an early bedtime after judging all day.

If driving yourself to the show, plan to be inside the show grounds at least one-half hour ahead of your scheduled assignment. When driving, remember safety. Park in well-lit areas. Walk out with someone if it is dark. Be alert. Carry a cell phone (but don't talk on it while walking to your car or when driving) or whatever new-fangled contraption has been developed. Use a GPS to find addresses. Web based map programs, such as MapQuest, help too. None of these are perfect, but the GPS comes closest. I love mine. I would marry mine if I weren't already married! (Actually, I am married to my former GPS—my husband!)

Be Prepared…for Anything

When you think of dog shows, especially outdoor shows, you may recall suffering from frigid winds, rain and snow, or the heat of a fiery furnace! So even though you'd like to minimize your luggage requirements, most judges are well advised to pack for every eventuality weather-wise. You may find that you are wrong most of the time anyway and learn to downsize, but you should always have a carry-on with vital necessities. For me, that means Standards, medications, show information, cell phone, wallet, a change of clothes, and entertainment to relieve airport and flight tedium. I have a carry-on bag with rollers, which is easier on your body than a bag you have to carry. With today's changing security requirements, I have bought several travel size items that will fit in a small plastic sealable bag to put in my carry on. Include a tag with your address and phone number both outside and inside each suitcase. If you wear a suitable judging outfit on your flight, you might be able to stuff all vital necessities in a small tote, but if your luggage does not arrive you may be ironing one outfit for two days of judging before your suitcase arrives—which if you are unlucky will arrive just in time to return home! I'd rather be prepared.

Here is something that has worked well for me over the years. I keep a suitcase packed with all the basic items and what I call an "oops kit" in my "launch" room. I wait to add clothes to suit the weather forecast until the day before departure. The oops kit contains band aids, corn pads, safety pins, aspirin, stomach soothers, flu and cold meds, etc. This kit might also include sleep aids for when your adrenaline keeps going after midnight, especially if you are faced with an early morning wake up call.

It's a good idea to pack some food items, such as fruit, granola bars, a cocoa packet, hard candies, peanuts, trail mix—whatever will get you through a delayed flight at an airport, sitting on the runway for four hours or reaching the motel at midnight, no restaurant on site, it's raining, and you have no car. Oh, yes…it happens. A candy bar and chips out of the vending machines do not make a great dinner. Believe me, I know.

Pack hand warmers in pockets and foot warmers into shoes, even indoor shows can be cold and drafty. I've never had much luck with the vacuum airless bags—and these present a problem coming home with no vacuum in the motel room. It would be awkward to chase down someone from housekeeping to help you pack. However, it does seem to help to pack things in mesh bags—sweaters and shirts in one, unmentionables in another, liquids and sprays in yet another. Plastic bags that zip shut also work.

Being prepared for outdoor shows takes a lot of thought. During the warmer months, sunscreen is important, along with a hat and shades. Wear light colors and outfits that are not lined. If need be, use one of the little fans that mist your face with water or one of the cooling hats, vests or neck/wrist bands. Bring packets of electrolytes, like Emergen-C™, or request some if it's torrid.

Exhibitors often wait to see what the judge wears in the heat. If the judge sheds a jacket, handlers will do the same. I don't want anyone passing out in my ring, so on extreme days, I tell them in advance, "Please feel free to remove your jackets." Some judges and handlers now wear a nice sport shirt in the dog days of summer. Clothes made from wicking material help an intolerable day be more tolerable. And forget the hottest creation known to womankind— pantyhose! One more thing ladies, before you head out to judge, take the time to look in a mirror while bending over—front and back—something you will be doing in the ring. It's embarrassing to be showcasing something you didn't mean to!

Obviously, you can't carry an umbrella while judging—or wear gloves. But you can choose your style of rain suits, coats, hats, boots, or duck shoes. Vanity should take a back seat when it comes to comfort. A roomy, sturdy coat (and hat) is the Renovere™ made in New Zealand. It comes in a convenient 12 x 6 bag, which fits compactly in your suitcase. Layers are good, either to shed or add on. Outfits are simple for men, usually a sport coat and pants, a tie and shirt. In extreme heat, wear a sun hat, lose the tie and, occasionally, golf shirts can offer a break in the routine. For the ladies, dresses, suits, and pantsuits are the norm. It's good to throw in an extra sweater or jacket—and, for outdoor spring and fall shows, long underwear. Washable microfiber is great and doesn't wrinkle. Silk squashes into the smallest corner and is easily washable. Both Travel Smith™ and Appleseed™ offer many selections for the frequent traveler.

Don't forget your feet since you will be on them up to eight hours a day, often on cement. Buying comfortable, sturdy, and attractive shoes designed for both walking and standing (judges do a lot of both) can be more difficult than finding the right dog! Brands suggested by my fellow judges include: SAS™, Clarks™, ECCO™, Dansko™, Munro™, Merrills™, Mephistos™, Easy Spirit™, Earth Shoes™, Arcopedia™, SoftSole™ (which has a soft egg carton type sole), Theresia M™, Merrell Primo Breeze™, Rockports™, Asgi™, and Cole Haan Nike Air™. Insoles such as Happy Feet™, Hydrosoles™, or even orthotics if you have foot problems, help the feet say ahhhhhhhhhhhhhh.

Money Considerations—Keeping Your Costs Down
A couple long-time judges scared me to death when I first began judging, telling me it cost them $10,000 to attain their first group. As a middle income person, I gulped and thought, "I can't do this." (I didn't dare ask whether that was for both of them or apiece—I was afraid to find out!)

Whether that $10,000 was accurate or not, it will certainly cost you some money to fulfill all the requirements to become a judge. The educational requirements are increasing and you may need to spend a considerable amount of money (and time) to obtain it. The period during which you are a provisional judge can be costly, but planning ahead helps. Now, if you are a "dog person" who is already going to lots of shows and attending seminars anyway, the additional costs might be minimal, but it can still amount to a pretty big investment. So I recommend that you focus on minimizing your costs so that you afford to reach your goals.

A great way to help save money, as mentioned above, is to get a frequent flyer credit card (shred your other cards!), which I use for groceries, department store purchases, postage—everything! I always try to use frequent flyer miles to travel to events where I estimate I won't cover my costs such as shows with minimal entries. For example, I was able to fly free to California for a show with just three entries—and for breed seminars. If possible, try to stay with one airline so the miles build up quickly. With the state of change in which airlines find themselves these days, some may start cutting back on their mileage plans. But until then, build them up and use them—frequently!

Like with airlines, you can take advantage of motel chains that offer "frequent stayer" cards as well. The idea is that the more you stay at a particular chain, the more benefits you will get including free or discounted room and meals. Sometimes you can earn frequent flyer miles as well if the chain has a relationship with your airline. Another option is to sign up with programs that offer discounted motel rates not linked to any one chain. Check out CheckInn Direct™, their web address is www.checkinncard.com. They charge a small annual fee, but the savings can add up. Sometimes it's worth the extra expense, however, to stay at the headquarters motel designated for the dog show as a matter of convenience. Another tip for finding bargains and things to do in strange cities: call Business Info at 1-800-466-4411 and you can find most restaurants/motels/museums/zoos/golf courses—whatever trips your trigger.

I personally prefer to drive rather than fly if the assignment is within six hours of home. For seminars and institutes, I would fly only when the event offered more than one breed to study. If you are going to drive and stay in a motel, consider bringing a cooler packed with drinks and goodies so you can avoid the costs of having to go out for meals all the time.

I also recommend that whenever possible you travel with someone. That way you can share some expenses and hopefully get the chance to enjoy some good company. Sometimes another judge would accompany me and share expenses—a chance to engage in good conversation as well! If you have to travel alone, try audio books for company. I've been able to do more reading than I have for years! Tip: the scarey ones keep you wide awake, and Dean Koontz's *Intensity* or Jeffrey Deaver's *The Bone Collector* keep you on the edge of your seat!

The more you travel and the more people you meet, the greater the likelihood you will make friends around the country. I often end up knowing someone in the area and am able to stay with them, saving on lodging and meals (just don't forget to reciprocate!). When that isn't possible, I try to find a roommate for a motel, making yet more friends. This adds to the fun, and we often talk dogs during the many hours spent together. By doing it this way, expenses often aren't any more than show weekends, and often less.

Getting Paid (Finally!)

Once you begin accepting judging assignments, you will start seeing money coming in after months or years of money only going out. The ironic thing, especially for new judges, is that they can be so focused on ring procedure and the mental challenges of sorting out dogs that they forget to turn in a bill for their hard work! Remember, you have put in years of effort to become a judge, you are good at what you do, and worth every penny you are owed. So don't be squeamish or shy about finances—unless you are independently wealthy, you probably can't afford to be a judge without getting paid!

New judges are generally paid a fee on a per-dog basis and/or some level of expense reimbursement based on your travel and lodging costs. If you've agreed on a per dog fee, this means the number of entries you've drawn, not how many appear in the ring. Paid expenses usually include meals, mileage (both usually at the IRS or US General Services Administration recommended rate) or airfare, motel, shuttle, and (rarely) a rental car. Expenses do not cover cleaning, a dog sitter, alcoholic drinks, goodies from the in-room bar, a new rain hat, or the chiropractor you visit for your aching back after the show! Judges who try to pad their bill may end up on the DNH (do not hire) list. Clubs are no dummies.

If a club pays expenses only, note that you will not make a "profit" on an assignment. The best you can do is break even. Depending on where you are in your judging career, you may be very willing to take on a judging assignment even if you do not break even on a financial basis. The opportunity to fulfill some requirement or gain some valuable experience may be very well worth it—like the newbie finally getting an opportunity to judge an entry of six Plott Hounds!

You may face the same decision if the club pays on the basis of per dog fee. Let's say the club offers you $3.00 a dog and you end up with 100 entries. In this case you would be paid $300. If you can hold your expenses to less than that, you will make money. However if you have to fly cross country to get to the show and spend three nights in a hotel, then obviously you won't. The math gets a bit more complicated if the club pays a combination of a per-dog fee and some expenses, but it is easier to figure out than most of the judging decisions you will face!

When a club calls you and asks you to judge their event, you will often hear something like "We pay $3.00 per dog—and we'll pay one night's lodging if you judge our puppy group." On the other hand, you may be asked, "What is your fee?" You need to know in advance what you will require, or at the very least ask what the club's usual payment policy is and then be prepared to accept or reject it. Judging fees are not set in stone and therefore it's sometimes difficult for a new judge to find out what's typical or reasonable. Check with judging friends who have progressed further than you have so you can have some idea of what is typical or not. When I was just starting out, if a club asked me what I charged, I told them that I preferred to have my expenses covered as the math usually would work better for me that way unless the show was very close to home. If they paid the traditional fee of so many dollars a dog, as most clubs do however, I had to determine how badly I wanted the assignment as most often the fee would not cover my expenses.

Once a judge becomes more experienced and is able to do half a group or more, some clubs are able and willing to pay more or to cover all travel expenses at a minimum. Recognize, however, just like judges and exhibitors, some clubs have deeper pockets than others. Even more experienced judges have to do the financial calculations and decide whether an assignment is worth having to float a loan to yourself to do it.

Prepare your bill according to your contract with the Club. Turn your bill into the Club Treasurer. The earlier the better, as occasionally the Treasurer cannot be found when you're ready to leave. When you receive your check, make sure it is signed (yes, sometimes a busy Treasurer forgets) and that it is made out for the correct amount. Sometimes you, or they, make mathematical errors.

Taxes

The Internal Revenue Service (and how is it a service, I question) is no longer a grandfatherly curmudgeon, and those of you dog show people who were able to treat your activities as a non-profit "hobby" on your tax returns need to tread carefully once you begin to earn fees as a judge. Obviously you should check with the IRS and/or a trusted accountant, but once you become a judge with consistent judging assignments and are regularly earning fees you will need to file as a business (Schedule C) and accurately record and report your income and expenditures. While this is a burden for most of us, businesses can claim legitimate losses that can help shelter other sources of income while a hobbyist can not claim losses to offset other income.

Keep a record book (see next section) and all receipts. For most judges, you may have substantial un-reimbursed travel expenses such as airfares, motels and the cost of parking. These are all legitimate deductions. The mileage and meal deduction rules change frequently, so check with the IRS and keep up-to-date so you can claim the right amount. Another important group of deductions relate to education requirements you need to meet in your judging profession including the costs of seminars, institutes, videos, and books. Dues for professional organizations, such as judging associations, may also be deducted. It's best to discuss any costs of gear or supplies (or other expenses you aren't sure about) with your tax professional. One thing for sure—if you've made a mistake in the ring or on your tax form, both the American Kennel Club and the Internal Revenue Service will find you!

Record Keeping

I highly recommend that new judges develop a record keeping system. There are at least four important reasons for you to keep good records:

1. For scheduling purposes and avoiding potential travel conflicts as were discussed above.

2. For accounting and tax purposes.

3. For your curriculum vitae, essentially a resume of your experience.

4. To keep track of your judging assignments.

Keep a file folder for your correspondence with a club, along with the contract. A check-off form is handy for noting when you receive show and hospitality information or make reservations. Be sure to obtain confirmation numbers when making reservations and a cell phone number from the club member designated to work with judges. Carry your contract, lodging and transportation information, and telephone numbers with you. This is what I include in my check-off form:

- Contract received : 4/28, Show Chair I.M. Perfect
- Show info: 10/30, cell: 555-OUR-DOGS
- Flight reservation made: 11/3 #_____
- Motel reservation: 1/5 #_____
- Shuttle reservation: 1/10 #_____
- Pick-up: At baggage claim Who_____

Schedules

For the purpose of scheduling and avoiding conflicts, create a spreadsheet with all of your assignments. You can keep this spreadsheet on a laptop or PDA or similar device so you can check it while you are traveling. Having immediate access to your schedule is helpful in case you get a call inquiring your availability. This way you can check not only for open dates, but make sure you do not have a conflict. If you are not that technically inclined, at least have a printed version of your schedule with you all the time, make notes on it, and then transfer or update the information when you get back home.

Following are some examples of the spreadsheets I maintain for record-keeping purposes.

Provisional Assignments

Show & Date	Curly Coated Retrievers	Flat Coated Retrievers	N.S. Duck Tolling Retrievers	Cocker Spaniels	English Cocker Spaniels	Field Spaniels	Spinoni Italiani	Vizslas
Friendly KC 2/10/08	*entry*					1		
Myhometown DFC 2/16/08	2	14	3	17	2	0	0	1
By-you KC 6/14/08	0	0	0	49			0	2
By-you KC 6/15/08						0		
Riverside KC 7/27/08				23	10	5	3	26
Riverside KC 7/28/08	6	8			3	1	4	38
Lake O' Sun 11/22/08		45						
Cactus Cluster KC 11/30/08	3	2	1	14	9	2	0	16
Total # of assignments in breed(s) with dogs present	3	4	2	4	4	4	2	5

Expense Record—March

Show	Air	Motel	Trans.	Mileage	Meals	Tips	Parking	Misc.
MO	260.00	180.00		25	13.98	3.00	15.00	
					32.00	6.00		
					9.90	2.00		
					18.89			
Hawaii	860.00	320.00	96		23.80	5.00	35.00	175.00*
			(rental)		19.42	4.00		(dogsitter)
					13.36	2.50		42.50*
					45.08	9.50		(cleaning)
						4.00		
KY		220.00		482	16.00	3.00		175.00*
					8.60	1.50		(formal)
					19.08	4.00		
					12.19	2.50		
					22.46	5.00		

*My own expense

Show Schedule

Date	Show	Locale	Breeds	Grp./Bis
Feb. 7	Capital City	DC	GSP, ACD, Beard, Mal, Can, 2 Coll. PON, Pul, SS	
Feb. 8	Capital City	DC	Ptr., GWP, Golden, Lab, BM, GD, Mas.	H
Feb. 9	Capital City	DC	An., GSMD, Kuv, Kom., Neo, PWD, Rott, Sam, Sibe	W
Feb. 10	Capital City	DC	3 Setters, Bern, BRT, Dobe, Gpin, Giant, Pyr	
Feb. 16	Tahiti	?	(gone 2/14-23)	
Feb. 17	Tahiti	?	all 3 groups	
Mar 15	Denmark	Copenhagen	Aus., GSD	
Mar 16	Denmark	Copenhagen	Bull., Pyr, Tib	
Mar 22	Riverside	River City, IA	T. Mas., all H exc. Aus., Beard, Coll.	H
Mar 23	Riverside	River City, IA	Mal., Bern., Blk, Box, BM, Dobe, GPin, Dane, Pyr., Kom, Neo, Port, Sam, Sib	W
Apr 4	Daisy	Yellowtown, KS	ACD, Beard, Beauc, BC, Bri, Can, Col, GSD, PON, Corgis	H
Apr 5	Daisy	Yellowtown, KS	3 Ptrs, Lab, 3 Setrs, Port, Rott, SS	BIS
Apr 6	Daisy	Yellowtown, KS	All W, exc. Mal, Box, Dobe, Dane, Mas, Port, Rott, Sam, OES, 3 Bel. Puli, Misc	W

Date	Show	Locale	Breeds	Grp./Bis
Apr 18	NCGFA	Topdog, USA	Goofenhound Ntl.	
Apr 24	NCGFA	Topdog, USA	Goofenhound Ntl.	
Apr 25	Myhometown KC	Hometown, IL	Minis	
Jun 14	Mad Hatter KC	Madtown, LA	Curly, Flat, Toller, Cock, Spin, Viz, Weim, Box	BIS
Jun 15	Mad Hatter KC	Madtown, LA	Ptr, GWP, GSP, GSP, Gold, Lab, Setrs, Field, all other W, most H	W, H, Jr
Jul 25	Daniel Boone	KY	Ak, Mai, An, BMD, BRT, Box, BM, Dob, DDB, GP, GD, Pyr, GSM, Kom, Kuv, NM, TM	W
Jul 26	Daniel Boone	KY	all H	
Jul 27	Daniel Boone	KY	AmC, EC, FS, Spin, Viz, Weim, Misc	H
Sept 6	3 Sisters	Sissyville, OH	Provisionals	
Sept 7	3 Sisters	Sissyville, OH		
Nov 14	Canterbury KA	Christchurch, NZ		
Nov 15	Canterbury KA	Christchurch, NZ		
Nov 22	Bythelake	Lake Co., IL	Dob, GP, GS, GD, all H	W
Nov 23	Bythelake	Lake Co., IL	Flat, Gold, Lab, Mas-TM	H, BIS
Nov 30	Cactus Town	Cactus Town, AZ	Provisionals	

Taxes

Your accountant or tax professional will really appreciate it if you can create a spreadsheet that shows all of your income and expenses. You can purchase an accounting program like QuickBooks™ or just develop a spreadsheet on your own. Once again, having this accessible on a laptop or other mobile device so you can enter data while on the road is helpful, especially if, like me, you tend to misplace receipts. These records aren't quite as good as receipts, but at least you'll have a record on one sheet, in addition to the receipts stuffed in your pocket, your wallet, your portfolio, and your suitcase.

Resume

I will discuss the importance of curriculum vitae/resume in Chapter 4, in the section on Moving Up to All Breeds. While having a record of all of your judging experience is something I recommend in any event, if you ever have desires to judge overseas you will need to have one. See page 64 for details.

Nuts and Bolts Tips—From Judges to Judges

- Be sure to obtain a written contract, not just a phone call or an e-mail.

- Obtain the cell phone number of someone in a position of authority from the club. Bring it with you, along with the correspondence from the club.

- Once you're judging several shows a year, travel agents might save you time and know your preferences as to seat, departure time, etc.

- Carry on medications, jewelry, and cash when flying. Wear something you could wear in the ring in case your luggage doesn't show up. Break in new shoes.

- Put I.D. inside your luggage as well as on the handle.

- A neck packet keeps your I.D. and tickets handy and secure.

- Wear a hat when it's hot and dress appropriately. Drink plenty of fluids. Remember sunglasses and sunscreen.

- Take hand and foot warmers along for cold-weather outdoor shows.

- Use a back-up alarm for a wake-up call or motel alarm.

- Focus on learning and use every opportunity to pick the brain of a knowledgeable breeder.

- Leave your suitcases at the Super's table or at hospitality, *not* in someone's car.

- Ask "Where's the restroom?"

- Check that someone is scheduled to take you to the airport and know where to meet that person.

- Ask who to turn your bill in to and remember to do it!

Chapter 3

IN THE RING

So the big day finally arrives, you are set to enter the ring as a judge for the first time. You have refreshed your memory by re-reading the breed Standard, watching the breed video until you can hum the theme by heart, and studying an Illustrated Standard. You know all you need to know about the idiosyncrasies of the breed, where the breed is strong, and where improvement is needed. The proper technique of handling your ring and the classes is firm in your mind. You know the big things—so let's talk about all the other stuff you need to know!

Groundwork

Upon entering the show grounds, check in at the Superintendent's desk, ask whether your judge's book will be at ringside and find the AKC representative. Provisional judges must be watched and evaluated by the AKC rep during several shows—at least three at this time. The rep will ask you how many times you've judged your provisional breed(s), so be prepared with that data. This will not be simple to come up with if you don't have good record keeping. Once you have progressed to the point of having several breeds, you may find yourself in the position of having judged Rottweilers six times, Tibetan Mastiffs once, Mastiffs five times, Dobermans three times, but you have yet to see a single cord of a Komondor.

It's a good idea to warn your club contact that you're new and would appreciate an experienced steward. Believe me, if you are assigned a new steward who needs training, it can slow you down. A new steward might do something like attempt to point out something in the Show Catalog. Of course if that happens, gently inform him or her that you're not allowed to see that information.

The entry at my first show was 165. Talk about baptism by fire! I'd been hoping for a moderate entry—40 or 50—enough for choices, but not overwhelming. I was concerned about staying on time, following procedure, and determining a pattern to follow in the classes. I took my husband (the World's Greatest Steward) with me and offered his services to the club, which they gratefully accepted. This way I wouldn't be hampered by training a first time steward, and he was especially good at keeping an eye on my time. By the way, staying on time, an average of three minutes per dog, is sometimes tricky for beginners. Avoid being like the judge who was told by the rep, "You *will* end this show before midnight!" Or the one who judged by headlights in a ring surrounded by cars.

Be at your ring about fifteen to twenty minutes ahead of start time. Greet your steward, and tell him or her your preferences—where you want the dogs set up, armband order or not, letting you know about a change of handlers, late arrivals for a class, how to inform you about absentees, dogs before bitches in Specials, and so on. Check the judge's book for move-ups and inform the steward. Ask the steward to double check your book for placements and absentees as we judges are not always perfect! It's a good idea to request your steward to keep the steward's book for six months and to request his or her contact information, in case of a question. Occasionally, the AKC will ask a judge to clarify a placement, and if your book is unreadable or unavailable, the steward's book will be a back-up.

Walk the ring to determine whether there is anything likely to trip a handler. If possible, correct a problem by asking to have a mat moved or re-taped—or warn handlers of any bottomless puddle, hill, or valley. Ask to have a hole or puddle filled. Pick up any debris in the ring that might be distracting to the dogs. You can request the Superintendent to enlarge your ring for a large entry or dogs who need more space to move. It doesn't always happen, but you can ask and at least tell exhibitors that you tried.

Your steward will ask what you'd like to drink and when you'll take pictures (after each time slot is recommended). New judges' assignments, particularly those with one breed, are sometimes scheduled during lunch breaks. If so, visit hospitality beforehand and ask if they'll serve you lunch early or if they can save you a plate. All clubs want to take good care of their judges. But it doesn't hurt to stick a granola bar or other snack in your judging bag just in case.

Skim your Standard again. The National anthem is played…then let the games begin!

The Judging Process

If you're like me, you'll be feeling a few butterflies the first time, but once you have your hands on the first dog, those butterflies fly away! After all, you've been ringside "judging" for many years—now you have the additional opportunity of hands-on judging: checking the bite; viewing eye color close up; feeling the depth of the ribcage; and determining length of loin through the coat. Even if quivering inwardly, hold that pointing finger steady! Putting on a confident demeanor helps you *become* confident.

Each judge will develop his or her own style and routine to reach their decisions. Your ring procedure is your choice, within certain guidelines, of course. You may walk the line, stand in the center to view the entire class, or send the dogs around immediately. The same procedure should be used whether it's a table breed or not, whether it's a single entry, or one of twenty. If you usually send the dogs around before examining, don't penalize the single entry or the table breeds by examining them first. Some dogs are nervous about the table, and going around once gives them a chance to calm down. Look for expression on the floor. The old saying goes, "Buy from the table, sell from the floor." Should you wish to examine a dog again, put him back on the table. Don't suddenly come at the dog like Goliath on David as that can bring on a fearful reaction on the part of the dog, especially the small ones.

When I started, I asked a fellow judge what steps she followed when judging, and she was kind enough to tell me her method. She said she walked the line, taking in type, saying to herself, "Hmmmm, I like 1, 3, and 6. Let's see how they move and hold up in examination." That worked for me then and I've used it ever since. A high percentage of the time, those dogs that fit my ideal picture of the breed show their style in movement and while I am going over them. Then all I have to do is sort out 1, 3 and 6—and find a 4th (sometimes the hardest job).

If you stick to type and your ideal of the Standard, you'll be happy when your winners walk into the ring. Exhibitors who are looking for consistency in a judge should be happy as well. Consistency doesn't necessarily mean your choices will look like cookie cutters, all the same size or color, but they might all have good shoulder layback or similar (and proper) proportions. Later on you may hear, "This one is that one's sister and that one's mother." That shows consistency. As Ann Rogers Clark always said, put the typey dogs at the front and sort out movement. It works—at least most of the time—since occasionally, a typey dog will show a soft back while going around, or I'll find a long loin or a mouth problem in the examination.

Once you have made your first initial cut based on your ideal of the Standard, move on to examine the dogs individually, paying particular attention to breed characteristics. For me, walking the line, doing an individual examination of all generalities (teeth, topline, testicles, etc.) and the pertinent breed specifics, then having each dog do a down-and-back, and lastly watching them go around works well. Does the Old English's topline rise to the rear? Is the muzzle strong and full and truncated? Is the Dachsie's keel (front) "strong, deep, long, and cleanly muscled?" Is the Pug a silver or apricot-fawn? Brush the hair away from the eyes on breeds like the Briard, Lhasa, or Skye Terrier so you can not only see the eye color and shape, but so the dog is aware of you. Lift the cords to feel the Puli's body. When examining the Chow or the Shar-Pei, say, "Teeth and tongue," to see the bite and the color of the tongue. Don't forget the bite and testicles. I also do a last-second check for muscle tone. Dogs should be in mint condition, maybe not with washboard abs, but in proper weight with good muscling.

Warning: Do not kneel in front of a dog. On the off chance that the dog is protective or frightened, your face will make the perfect target. Even if the dog is well behaved, the AKC rep will likely slap your wrist for doing it. And that could be worse! In fact, it's not a good idea to kneel by a dog at all—not only does it make you vulnerable, but, oh, the leg cramps that night!

View each dog's gait coming and going, and from the side, whether in a triangular or down-and-back pattern, followed by going around. Profile, temperament, and movement should all speak to you defining type: This *is* a Lakeland Terrier. It *is not* a Welsh Terrier or, heaven forbid, an Airedale! Although the type vs. soundness discussion is always a hot topic, remember once you've found type, you can look for soundness. *No* Standard calls for a dog to be unsound.

Unsound movement means type is not ideal as it is a deviation in structure. Unsound temperament is also undesirable. Type and soundness together equal the total. Some breeds place a heavy emphasis on the profile, others do the same on movement.

Now you can sort the dogs in the order you prefer. You may either make the placements then or send them around again, one at a time or all together. If necessary, make adjustments to the placements and point, saying clearly One-Two-Three-Four. Every now and then someone becomes confused, so it's up to you to remember which order they should be in as you mark your book and hand out the ribbons.

Unless there are dogs in the class that are very close in quality and you are still undecided, there is no reason to continue moving the dogs or going over them individually. The old saying is true, "They don't get any better." And the one you like may actually get worse—or step in a hole!

Always take the comfort and safety of the dogs into consideration. Handlers will be grateful (though probably not eternally) when you are considerate of them as well. If the ring is small, put one group against one side, or better yet, allow them to leave the ring while you judge the other section.

Judging the Whole Dog

Many times, when we begin showing, we tend to say, "That dog has the better rear" or "My dog's color is the best." However, knowing what makes a Pointer a better Pointer, not just the rear or color, is what separates the in-ring judges from the ringside judges. So one of the most important skills for you to develop is the ability to judge the dog as a whole. Being able to evaluate a poor Chow from a good one is not what it takes to make a discerning judge, but to compare two, or twenty, good Chows, or to sort out a class of average dogs, is a chance to make yourself shine.

In contrast to judging the whole dog, some people focus on fault judging. That method might find you following a trail that ends at mediocrity. Every dog has faults, some more obvious than others, some more serious than others. Although a dog may be faulty in one area, he may be so superior in another that he deserves the blue, if not the purple or even the purple and gold. I prefer to reward the whole dog, not punish one or two faults. So when someone says, "How could she put up a dog that is missing two teeth?" you can be content in your knowledge that the winner had a vital requirement for breed type or a characteristic that is sorely lacking in the breed.

You must have an ideal in your mind. Compare the dogs, finding the one that most closely fits this dream dog. When weighing one body part against another, it is difficult to determine which is more important. Pondering about this can stump a judge. If this occurs, think back to breed characteristics—is the "part" something that defines a breed? Will it hamper or help breed function? Perhaps the fact that one dog's tail carriage is not ideal is less important than the fact that its muzzle and jaws are deep enough to carry a goose, as compared to the entry that has a tail which flows beautifully off the topline, but that is weaker in the muzzle.

Grooming is the frosting on the cake. We're judging the whole dog, but sometimes a great, correct grooming job does make the cake extra yummy!

Judging Large Classes

When judging a large class of dogs, a judge may divide the class and make cuts after evaluating each section. Dividing a class into two or more sections is not as intimidating as trying to sort out twenty or more dogs. It's also more appealing to spectators who can observe which entries are the most pleasing to you. The exhibitors also appreciate not having to go around ten times or to stand in the pouring rain or blazing sun for half an hour or more. Just because you have to brave the elements doesn't mean everyone else should have to!

Find a method that suits you. Some judges use a marker dog and place the ones they like ahead of that dog and the ones they don't behind him. A few put the "keepers" on one side of the ring—or send them out of the ring, making a note as to which should return. You may send the others around to give them a second look. Or you can sort them out as they go, saying "Go to second, please," or "Go to the front, please." A simple "Thank you" suffices for those that are to go around to the end of the line. You'll then take your elite and work with them again, sorting them out into the proper placements.

As the AKC recommends, keep five from the first group because there may not be anything as good in the other, and it's possible one could go lame during the competition. If you don't do this, you could wind up in the embarrassing position of having three dogs to place from a class of ten.

If you have sent some dogs outside the ring, please don't forget about them as I've seen happen! This is very embarrassing and will draw howls of protest from those outside. This brings us back to the value of a good steward, who won't allow you to have an oversight like that. Whatever you do, do *not* dismiss either the Winners Dog and the Winners Bitch from the ring until you award Best of Winners. There cannot be a Best without two competing!

So while having a large class of dogs may be more work for you, it also gives you more choices and makes it more stimulating and fun!

Handling Problems and Disqualifications

Whether it's a child, a friend, or the same handler who, for the fifth time, you must disappoint, remember you are there only to find the best dog in your opinion. Judges must develop a thick skin. This is particularly important when you have to deal with handling problems and disqualifications, part of your responsibility as a judge beyond trying to determine which dog is best.

It's your decision whether to let in late arrivals. Most judges allow latecomers to place their dogs at the end of the line behind the dogs that have not been examined—but it's up to you. It's also up to you to if an exhibitor asks whether his single entry breed can be switched to a different time. Try to be flexible and cooperative—exhibitors appreciate it!

Temperament problems can vary from shyness to threats to attacks, and your response can range from an excusal to a disqualification. If the dog is so shy that you cannot examine him, excuse him from the ring—marking your book accordingly. For example, "Exc., could not examine," with your initials. If there appears to be a good reason for a dog to be reactive (such as a sudden loud noise), you may decide to allow the dog to stay in but not place it, give some leeway, or withhold. It's at your discretion, but be prepared to defend your position if questioned. When a dog growls or threatens you, the handler, another exhibitor, or another entry, he should be excused—again marking your book appropriately.

An attack or attempt to bite definitely means a disqualification (DQ). Don't jeopardize anyone by allowing the dog to stay in. This means any dog from an Irish Wolfhound, to a Beagle, to a Maltese—the size doesn't matter or forgive the behavior. Call for the AKC rep, fill out the papers, mark your book (DQ, attack, your initials) and explain the situation to the handler—the dog cannot be shown again until such time as he may be reinstated. You'll receive a letter from the AKC asking whether the dog should be considered for reinstatement or not. You might say yes if, for instance, the dog had just been stung by a bee or bitten by another dog in the ring.

Even judges are occasionally intimidated by certain dogs. Animals pick up on tingling nerves, so approach each dog with confidence. Never approach from the rear. Allow the dog to see you. Speak to the handler, saying "Good morning," or something similar. Do a smooth examination (i.e., keep a hand on the dog at all times). It's advisable, particularly with the guard dog breeds, to keep a hand on the dog's neck or withers so you can feel if he starts to turn his head. When studying these breeds, watch a breeder go over a dog. How is the approach? Where does he keep his hands? Learning the best way to work with each breed should be part of your training and education.

If you sense nervousness on the part of the dog or the handler, ask the handler to hold the dog's head still while you go over the body. When finished with the examination, it's a good idea to walk around the back of the dog, rather than toward the head. People can be bitten at any time, even accidentally by their own dog. Judges should make it a practice to have a tetanus shot and keep it updated every five years.

If a dog has a breed standard disqualification and it's obvious (color, bite, etc.), mark in your book "DQ," the reason, and initial. If you question the size or weight as a DQ, you must call for the appropriate wicket or scale (having practiced the proper procedure several times) before marking the dog in or out.

Most dogs are well-trained and accepting of an examination. People, on the contrary, are not always so well-behaved. Defuse a touchy situation with exhibitors or owners as calmly as possible. If poor behavior, name calling, or poor sportsmanship continues, call for the AKC rep or the Show Chairman to request a bench show committee. The bench show committee is made up of officials from the club, who will determine what the penalty will be. The AKC rep will be present, and the accused may be present to give a response.

Withholding Ribbons

A judge may withhold ribbons at any time—during the classes, Winners, or Best of Breed. Within the classes, my personal criteria is to ask myself the "duck questions," substituting the breed of dog for the word duck. Does it look like a _____? Does it walk like a _____? Does it quack like a _____ (quack meaning temperament)? If I can't tell whether it's a Siberian Husky or an Alaskan Malamute, I withhold in the classes. If a German Shepherd Dog is shy, I withhold. If it looks like the breed and has good temperament, but is geeky, bouncing like a Kong™ from here to there never knowing where the dog might land, or simply is not worthy of a Championship, I withhold in Winners.

Be gentle. These dogs are often handled by novices who adore their dogs. Say something like, "I'm sorry, but your dog needs to grow up (or learn to work with you or whatever), so today I am withholding Winners." If the dog has no redeeming qualities, find out why they bought their dog. If the answer is as a friend, say, "You've got a wonderful friend. You make a good team, but if your goal is a Championship, search out a really good breeder." Your advice and encouragement might produce a future dedicated fancier.

Occasionally a wonderful dog is made less so by handling errors. Giving a bit of advice might make the difference on whether that exhibitor enters another show. That's true even if the dog isn't a great one. Take a second to tell them to set up the dog in a more moderate manner or to use a loose leash.

Mental Challenges

Judges are in the ring to reward attributes, not to fault judge. Rewarding attributes is a difficult mental challenge, especially for the new judge. It's much easier to think, "This dog's tail is too short," than to find the youngster who stands out like a beacon in a fog. Most ringside judges are astute at fault finding. Every judge has heard someone complain, "How could you put up that dog? His eyes are too light!" "Well, because he has the sweetest expression, the good tight feet that are lacking in the breed, and the best shoulder I've seen in ages."

Early in my judging career, I found myself standing and staring at two bitches, comparing a better croup to a better shoulder. As I heard someone murmur, "She's having trouble making up her mind." I thought, "They aren't going to change. Let's send them around again and see who moves more smoothly." I made my placement and was content. I could've done that five minutes before if I'd gone back to form and function. I've remembered that ever since. Just look for the best overall dog.

Marking Your Book

Thoroughly re-read the AKC's *Guidelines for Conformation Judges* regarding the marking of your judge's book. Make a dot or small check in front of (not on the number) each dog that is present. If in doubt about something, ask the AKC Rep. Even veteran judges make the occasional mistake or a never before experienced circumstance occurs, and you get thrown for a loop. Such red-face incidents might include examining the first dog twice, forgetting to go over one at all, or awarding a ribbon but marking it incorrectly in your book. Try to remember the first handler's number or outfit, or count the number in the class, and look at armbands when making placements to avoid such miscues. Before long, marking your book will be second nature. Until then, check and double check.

The Superintendent will catch most mistakes and ask you to make a correction. Any correction/change must be initialed in your judge's book. If all else fails, the AKC will catch an error that slips past everyone else. But it's best to avoid embarrassing goofs.

At the End of the Day

When you're totally finished with your assignment for the day, turn in your judge's book to the Superintendent. When you do this, you can ask for your catalog and pink sheets (your copy from the judge's book). *Do NOT, ever, ever, ever forget to turn in your book!* Not only will this hurt the evaluation done on you, it will mess up the records that the AKC Rep and Superintendent are required to keep as well. You don't want to get on the wrong side of either one!

If you're a provisional (whether a newbie or finishing your last breeds to become an all-breed judge), check with the AKC Rep about your evaluation. Hopefully, it will be a good one. If not, don't whine or become angry, tempting as that may be. Discuss it with the rep, giving your reasons for your decisions, noting them on the evaluation sheet. Don't wait until the next day or next week. By then, the rep's evaluation has already been sent to the AKC Judges Department.

A Quick Character Test for Judges

Along with expertise, a judge needs to be ethical and show character. Here's a quick test and how I would answer these questions that relate to ethics and character.

- What do you do when the same handler has the best dog in each class? *Place it at the head of the line.*

- What do you do when a dog is gorgeous standing and then it falls apart when it moves? *You weep inwardly and place it where it belongs in the class.*

- What do you do when you have several top winning dogs in a class or a group? *You place the ones that are best on that day. You only have to make yourself happy—no one else!*

- What do you do if there's a question in your mind as to the dog's size or weight? *Call for the wicket or the scale. Use the wicket on a flat surface—a table, cement floor, or a ramp.*

- What do you do when extreme trimming is faulted in the Standard? *It is considered a fault like any of the others mentioned.*

- What do you do when a Standard calls for docking and/or cropping, but a dog with a natural tail or ears is entered? *We will be seeing more and more of this as many countries now forbid these practices. You follow the Standard. If a Standard does not define the cosmetic surgery clearly, it is up to the judge whether or not to judge, excuse, or withhold.*

- What do you do with a "may be tabled" or "may be shown on a ramp" breed? *Follow the Breed Club's recommendation.*

- What do you do when a pleasant person comes into multiple classes with entries you cannot place or must place at the end of the line? *Pray that person will have at least one entry that you can happily place over another.*

- What do you do when a dog is entered in two classes? (This will happen to you sooner or later.) Sometimes novices simply make a mistake or two different owners/handlers enter the dog. What do you do? *Be ready to advise your steward and the exhibitor. If the dog loses in one class, it cannot go into winners even if it won the other class. Once the dog is shown in the first class, it **must** compete in the second class. So the best thing to do is for the handler to declare the dog absent from the first class and show it in the second.*

- Many people talk about balance, but if that means an equally poor rear to match the awful front, all that gives you is a poor, but balanced dog—or at best a mediocre dog. Does that dog win? *No. Judges don't fight travel delays, inclement weather, and long days on our feet in order to reward mediocrity.*

Lessons From a Veteran—Me!

Based on my experience, here are some lessons I've learned that should be of help to new judges.

- Don't go out to be a "giant killer." But if a puppy deserves BOB over the specials, do it. Have the courage of your convictions. Remember, that evening you will have to look yourself in the mirror.

- It's difficult to throw out the best dog structurally for cosmetic faults. Take your choice of several options. When a Beardie's part is too "knitting needle" perfect, I take great joy in messing it up. I've also told people to brush out the "starch." When you find color on your hands, you can excuse the dog for foreign substance or, if you don't know which dog in the class is the guilty party, say loudly, "Look at this…my hands are orange!" You can keep a superior dog in a cut or two, making a statement by obviously examining the trimmed coat, and then excusing it before the final judging. Another choice is to make a statement as you award the placement. Say, "Never bring a dog in this condition under me again."

- Someone told me once that a particular dog "had the best shoulder she ever felt." I responded, "But he doesn't use it." She said, "But he'll produce it." Me again: "No he won't." A shoulder isn't just bone, but ligaments and muscles—and that magic ingredient: *heart!*

- The German Shepherd Dog Club of America requests that a temperament test be done on each entry. Good for them, I say! The club sends a pamphlet on how to conduct this to each judge. A new Shepherd judge should also watch a breeder judge perform this properly. If you do not do the temperament test when you judge Shepherds, you may still judge the breed, but you'll lose the respect of the serious fanciers.

- Judges come in two varieties—the artists and the engineers. The artist pictures the ideal and sees what comes closest. The engineer measures and feels. The artists may be able to make a quicker decision, but a hands-on examination is important too. The best is a combination of both, finding that ideal and confirming the decision with your hands.

- Be flexible in procedure when the temperature changes or the sun heats up. Also, be willing to change your method in running a group of Salukis, or Malamutes, or Maltese around.

- In examining the mouths of Toy breeds, gently cup the head and lift the lips with your thumbs. The Pug's bite can be felt by running your thumb over the teeth.

- When counting teeth, learn to count them in groups: 3-4-1-2 (each side of the upper jaw); 3-4-1-3 (each side of the lower jaw), totaling 42. With a few breeds, it's easiest to look at bite, sides, and then say "Open" to see the rest.

- Breeds, like hemlines, go up and down. Some years several Goosendorf Hounds are worthy of BIS. Other years, the breed is lacking in quality.

- If there are holes in the Standard, talk to your mentor. Study the Illustrated Standard if there is one or the AKC video. These often fill in holes.

- Remember to look for certain faults or drags of the breed which are becoming widespread: short upper arms, long hocks, low on leg, and upright shoulders. Sometimes we have few choices, but when possible, avoid rewarding universal problems.

- When studying new breeds, remember breed specific qualities. I will never forget being told that Portuguese Water Dogs should have buns of steel. That terrific muscle tone gives them the push to dive into the water.

- Does the dog look like, act like, and move like the breed? That's type.

- Even in breeds that do not prioritize head qualities, the head often defines the breed.

- Nothing looks just like an Old English Sheepdog, not even his "kissing cousins," the Beardie, or the Polish Lowland Sheepdogs.

- If you have a large entry, relax, and enjoy. They're easier than small entries!

- If in doubt, remember function.

- Reward a quality that's difficult to achieve in the breed.

- If they're built right, they should move right.

- You'll never find a dog with all ideal characteristics. Searching for it is what is fun. And when it comes close, oh, how your heart zings!

In the Ring Tips—From Judges to Judges

- Keep in shape. Judging is a physical activity. If you are physically challenged in some way, practice going over dogs and moving about so that you don't lose your balance.

- Check to see if you're judging the Miscellaneous breeds or Best In Show, so that you bring the appropriate Standards. Refresh your memory by reading the Standards, viewing the breed video, and/or talking to a mentor.

- Don't be nervous or feel intimidated by the AKC Reps. They are there to assist you and give you valuable feedback.

- Learn breed specifics and evaluate them properly.

- Keep your Standards on the table for quick reference.

- Ask for the wicket, if questioning size. For breeds with size disqualifications, carry a steel tape measure to check the height on the wicket before you show the wicket to the exhibitor and proceed to measure the height.

- Aim to judge like a specialist in every breed.

- Be passionate about judging—even when standing in 105 degree heat or 32 degree sleet.

- Wear comfortable shoes. Some judges advise changing shoes mid-day or before groups.

- Avoid jewelry that might fall in the dogs' faces. Pin ties and scarves.

- Check placement of the table for convenience in marking your book.

- Check the armbands yourself. Don't depend on your steward.

- Be consistent.

- Keep your mind open and your mouth shut.

- Practice your poker face—no looks of horror at a dog!

- SMILE!!!

- When finished examining, get on with it—they don't improve.

- No need for a massage on a shorthaired dog. What you see is pretty much what you get.

- On coated breeds, feel under the coat.

- If timid about a breed, don't judge it. Be direct in your approach.

- Be patient with puppies and new exhibitors.

- Be friendly and courteous to all exhibitors.

- Have a sense of humor.

- Be gentle with all dogs, but especially so with Toys and puppies.

- Little dogs can and should move well!

- Encourage newcomers to the sport.

- Remember your mother's instructions—say "please" and "thank you." And never be rude!

- Control your ring without being a dictator.

- Give exhibitors enough time (within reason) to set up their dogs.

- Give instructions clearly.

- Check for full dentition when the Standard calls for it.

- Show everyone the same courtesy in examination and watching, even if it's the ugliest dog you've ever seen.

- Don't tolerate poor temperament—in either dogs or people.

- Watch the *dog* as it gaits, not the spectators or another ring.

- If you send two dogs around together, switch the dogs' positions for a second lap.

- Have a reason for every placement.

- If asked why their dog didn't win, ask them to describe their dog. Often they will come up with the reason themselves.

- If asked, say something nice about the dog—find something: beautiful eyes, good temperament! Then follow up with the reason the other dog won.

- Do not penalize a dog for being appropriately reserved for its breed.

- Look for what is correct according to the Standard, not necessarily what you prefer, i.e., you like rectangular structure, but the breed is supposed to be square.

- Check your judge's book over to make sure things are correctly marked and signed, and remember to turn it in!

- Pick up your pink sheets and catalog.

- Do not snarl, growl, or lift your lip.

- Don't take criticism personally.

- Go easy on praising dogs and do not denigrate one either.

- Don't make comparisons, but saying something like, "Nice youngster" or "Another day" is fine.

- Don't "pad" your expenses. The Show Committee knows when you're fudging, and your name goes to the top of the Black List.

- Do look at your check to make sure the amount is correct and that it is signed!

- Treat your steward like an angel and they will treat you like a god(dess).

- You have been invited to judge because you are thought highly of in the world of dogs, but don't think you're the star of the show. It is just a dog show—your judging will be over at the end of the day, and the exhibitors are already looking toward the next week's judges.

- Enjoy yourself!!!

- Most of all, be true to yourself. You're the person you see when you look in the mirror.

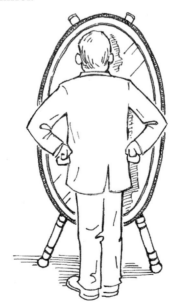

A long-time judge gave me this good advice: "Make your mistakes quickly. At least it will look like you believe you know what you're doing!"

Chapter 4

MOVING UP TO ALL BREEDS AND MORE

Eventually you will finish your provisional assignments. Your first breed, your breed of origin, has been a good introduction to judging. You are confident of your breed knowledge and have had some experience in judging numerous dogs at matches, sweepstakes, and futurities. You've learned how to sort through the dogs and determining your placements has not been a problem.

You've gone through typical learning pains in establishing your procedures, but you are confident of your abilities and that, as time goes on, you'll find ways to perfect your process and smooth out any kinks.

Some of you will wish to remain breed specialists and stay right where you are. A few of you will want to add just one or two more breeds, ones you have been closely associated with, either through ownership yourself or with good friends. Others of you will want to climb through the ranks, adding breeds to become group or multi-group judges. A few of you with the highest aspirations will want to become an all-breed judge. A word of advice to that select group—start young!

Applying for Additional Breeds

The application requirements relating to gaining approval to judge additional breeds is available online from the AKC and is different from that for your first breed. Once again, it involves proving you have the expertise to judge through a combination of educational efforts, the mentoring you have received, attending specialties, ringside observations, judging at matches, etc. If you have one original breed, you may apply for one additional. If you started with two, you may apply for two additional breeds. On the third and fourth applications, you may apply for as many additional breeds as you're approved for at the time, i.e., if two, two additional; if four, four additional. Once you reach your fifth application, you may apply for up to fourteen breeds which is the maximum you may apply for at one time. But that doesn't mean you'll be allowed that many! You will need to complete at least five provisional assignments in each new breed with observations by at least three different AKC Representatives. Check the AKC website for full details.

Continue Your Homework

Breeder judges remain the true experts on their breeds. However, shows depend on multi-breed judges to fill out their panels. A non-breeder judge may never have a breeder's depth of knowledge, but we can all strive to learn the fine points of each breed. The key is to keep studying. There's never a better time than the present to begin learning about additional breeds. It's best to concentrate on progressing within your group rather than leaping into another this early in the game. Here are several approaches to the subject of additional breeds:

1. Work toward a breed you know fairly well already, perhaps one you owned but didn't qualify for as a breed of origin. Another possibility is a close friend's breed. Friends trade a lot of information about their breeds and, in fact, often help one another out at shows (prior to becoming a judge, that is).

2. Work toward a breed that consistently draws high numbers of entries. This is particularly true if your first breed is numerically challenged. Larger entries make you more visible at shows and can make a judge more appealing to Show Chairs. In addition, while zipping around the country for $3-4 a dog, it helps financially.

3. Work toward a breed that you have the opportunity to obtain education on (i.e., a nearby mentor, several regional specialties in your area, or possible sweepstakes assignments).

If you believe you will want to continue on to become eligible to judge additional breeds, continue your education *while* you are doing your provisionals. Discuss breeds with other judges and veteran breeders. Write for or download the application for additional breeds, so that you can fill it out as you gain knowledge and complete the required educational experiences.

As a beginning judge, your assignments will often allow you time to study other breeds and gain mentors at the shows you attend. That's where you can always find knowledgeable dog people clustered together. It's always fun, as well as helpful, to "talk dogs." If specialties are held in conjunction with the show, it's well worth staying an extra night or two to sit ringside and drink in the knowledge of veteran breeders. Occasionally seminars are given at shows.

Attending specialties as an observer gives you the best opportunity to see many good dogs. National specialties draw the breed's crème de la crème. Long-time breeders may be available to mentor you. But even most regional specialties boast a good number of quality entries. While you should not feel obligated to fly around the country to attend a National for every breed you are interested in (especially when there are Regionals held nearby), recognize that Nationals remain the best place to see the highest quality dogs and to learn from the best mentors.

Clubs occasionally offer Best Puppy, Bred-by Exhibitor, or other competition during their shows. Sometimes a match is held following the show. Volunteer and pick up the experience you need to become qualified for additional breeds. The judges who have been on their feet all day evaluating 175 dogs, plus two groups, don't want to do the "extras." Believe me!

Specialties

Regional specialty clubs often seek out provisional breeder judges who are in the process of meeting their requirements. These shows are exciting because they tend to draw numbers of good quality dogs. They're also more relaxed, without the tight time restrictions of all-breed shows. You may also get a chance, especially at National specialties, to bolster your judging experience because of the many different types of classes offered, including many seldom seen at All Breed shows. For example, Best Bred-By, Best Puppy, and Veterans are typically offered. Veterans are my favorite. Not only do we get to see history passing before our eyes, but the thrill of seeing these oldsters is always moving. Pride glistens in owners' eyes, and the dogs preen, once again strutting their stuff.

At specialties, altered veterans may compete for BOB. At all-breed shows, intact veterans may show before Champions (Specials) and compete in BOB. If they are altered, they are shown after BOB.

Other classes offered might include Brace, Brood Bitch, Stud Dog, Field Tested, or Herding Titled and more are the order of the day at specialties and provide you unique and valuable judging opportunities. Familiarize yourself with the guidelines in judging these classes. Braces are two dogs, usually similar in appearance. It's quite striking when they gait in unison. Stud Dog and Brood Bitch classes include the parent with two progeny. I like to see the best characteristics of the parent exhibited by the get. Hopefully, they are an improvement over the parent as this is our goal as breeders. The parent needs to be examined only for disqualifications.

AKC reps seldom attend specialty shows. If you need more evaluations for approval following your provisional assignments or before applying for additional breeds, it might be best to call the Judges Operations Department and ask for suggestions on obtaining those.

Groups

It normally takes several years to get approval to judge every breed in a Group, which is the prerequisite for Group judging. After completing your fifth application, you may apply for all the remaining breeds in a Group subject to the current limit of fourteen breeds per application.

Group judging is different in that many times you will have had several (or all) of the dogs earlier in the day. In those cases, you usually need to only do a quick once-over in the Group ring. Then send the dog down and back (they don't always need to run the entire distance—sometimes you can hardly see that far!) around to the end, and on to the next dog.

As I'm examining the dogs, I try to sort out the possible winners in my mind. Besides being around dogs and dog people, the mental challenge of judging Group is my favorite thing. I might be thinking Boxer, Bernese, Akita, Dane and then change it to Standard Schnauzer, Boxer, Bernese, Akita. I may decide to keep the Dane in the running, along with the Tibetan Mastiff.

At this point, several scenarios can occur. Usually the judge pulls out six (never five—again, it's a lonely walk out by yourself). Dismiss the others in the Group with thanks, gait the six individually again and then make placements.

Another method is the judge may simply place four. These two methods are usually the most expedient. A longer, more involved method is to run the entire Group together or individually and then make a decision.

Once you are a Group judge, you are more marketable and can expect to receive more invitations to judge. Your judging day will be a lot longer, that's for sure! Once you have this degree of experience, you are more likely to be asked to judge at Nationals, even overseas, or on TV!

Also, once judges are approved for one Group, they may judge the Miscellaneous breeds. Study the Standards the AKC will send you. If possible, talk to breeders, attend a seminar, and read articles or books to learn as much as possible about these interesting breeds. New breeds are entering Miscellaneous as fast as they can go through the revolving door at the AKC!

Best In Show

Currently after having judged your initial Group ten times, you may request approval for Best In Show (BIS). Ideally, you would know everything about every breed before taking on this task. But in practical terms, with as many shows that are held in the U.S. each weekend, more BIS judges are needed than the current two dozen or so who actually are approved to judge every breed.

While waiting to walk into that center ring with only seven dogs, read the Standards of the Group winners. Talk to knowledgeable Group judges about the procedure of evaluating breeds that are less familiar to you. You may have questions such as how do you go over a Poodle, for instance, if you're a Terrier judge. Or you might ask what makes an outstanding Buhund.

The late Raymond Oppenheimer, a knowledgeable Bull Terrier breeder and judge, once suggested that when judges first begin their career, they should start with Best In Show. Here one has seven outstanding examples of their individual breeds. It would be difficult for a judge to go wrong! After they have experience with BIS, they could move on to the groups, where there might be 20-30 outstanding examples of the breeds and, eventually, on to the individual breeds.

Nationals

The ultimate honor for any judge is to be asked to do a National Specialty show. Some Nationals attract so many entries that they are spread over several days. Bitches, dogs, and Best of Breed may be assigned to three different judges. These shows are thrilling because the best of the best walk into your ring, asking for your opinion, and hoping for your nod.

We are often asked to choose Awards of Merit (AOMs) at specialties, and it's become customary at Nationals. These are "runners up" to the Best of Breed and Best of Opposite, dogs that on another day might have worn the crown. A certain percentage of the entries are chosen, and you will be informed of the number prior to judging Best of Breed. It's up to the club whether these are done in order and whether Best Of Opposite Sex (BOS) and Best Of Winners (BOW) are to be included in the AOMs.

Critiques are the order of the day at Nationals (and often at Regionals), so school yourself on using breed specific terms. Carry a notebook, a tape recorder, or video camera to make notes. Later when you arrive home to write the critique, use the Standard for phrases that describe the breed specifics.

Junior Showmanship

A judge who has gone beyond Provisional status and has been approved for at least one breed can apply to judge Junior Showmanship. You must also show that you have had some relevant experience like having been a handler, showing in Juniors as a youngster, or perhaps having had children in the sport. Obviously you should enjoy helping these future handlers and be familiar with the rules of Junior Showmanship. The better you handle this job, the more entries you will attract.

A desire to judge Juniors can really help make a judge be more marketable to a club, especially for specialties. These clubs would have to hire an additional judge if their breed judge is not approved for Juniors. A judge may also request to preside over Junior Showmanship at specialties only.

The priority in Juniors is to concentrate on the handler's abilities, rather than the quality of the dog. When the class begins, sort the dogs out according to size and speed of gait, or you may ask the juniors to do this themselves. The juniors' safety should be foremost in your mind. Sort them out so that bigger, faster dogs are in the front. Juniors are usually very efficient at this! Make sure there is no crowding when the class goes around. If a junior is having trouble handling a large or dominant dog, stop the class and excuse the child. Do explain to both the parents and the junior that the excusal was only for safety reasons. If either are concerned this might happen, another eligible dog may be substituted for the entry one half hour before Junior Showmanship is scheduled.

If the class is large, it can be split, perhaps into large breeds and smaller ones. Keep at least five out of the first group in case an entry has to be excused. Add one or more from the second section, so that when you award four placements, the fifth child doesn't have a long, lonely walk out of the ring. This is similar to what you would do in the breed ring.

I find these classes more challenging than any in the breed ring. These youngsters are good and would out-handle me on my best day! The procedures you use in the ring must conform to what you would do in breed judging, i.e., no questions, no circling around the dog, no unusual patterns. That means no X's!

The best advice I received when I starting judging Juniors was to look for the junior handler who is so smooth that you would love to have them handle for you. Do you notice jerky or exaggerated movements? A handler should blend into the background. Watch for exhibitors who listen closely and ask for clarification if they don't understand, rather than do something wrong. In addition, a friend gave me a tip to look for the child who has to work, but manages to do it without a lot of fuss. Perhaps the dog won't show expression or pulls too hard. Or it doesn't stack like a robot. Your winner may be the child who has to keep resetting the feet, but does so quickly and without losing patience.

On a cold, rainy day in Montana, a Junior quietly reached out of the ring and grabbed a blanket to wrap his Chinese Crested in during examinations of the other dogs. In my estimation, he cared more about the dog than the win. With his other skills, that second of compassion gave him the win.

I also like to see a rapport between the Junior and the dog. I'd like to have an idea that a relationship really exists between the team, not the idea that Mom did the grooming, Dad did the training, and Junior would rather be playing basketball and doesn't even particularly like the dog!

Because Junior Showmanship should be an educational experience, many will ask you how they can improve. (Note the positive question, rather than the negative "What did I do wrong?"). You can provide some positive guidance by taking a moment or two at the end of the class to give suggestions and cheer their efforts. You might also want to give a reason for your top selections. Many adults could learn from these polite, sincere, and efficient youngsters!

You're on TV!

The day may come when you are invited to do a televised group show. Often these are formal affairs. That means tuxes for the men and formal dress for the ladies. Practice walking in the shoes you choose for your debut! Most of these events are taped and shown on TV at a later time, so should the worst case scenario occur, your tumble can be edited out. Whether live or taped, the crew will inform you of particulars, such as where to stand, how many to keep in your cut, and so on. Don't showcase and keep more dogs than they say. It can affect the length of the program.

Remember this is all about showing off the dogs, but it doesn't hurt to look your best yourself! Check for smeared mascara or a sprig of spinach in your teeth.

Foreign Invitations

Judges don't have to be approved for a great number of breeds before they may start receiving foreign invitations. While breeder judges with sterling reputations may be more apt to receive a call, most foreign clubs are looking primarily for lots of experience in several breeds.

Different countries will vary as to the types of contracts, procedures, requirements, and financial compensation they use. Most will ask for your curriculum vitae/resume as mentioned earlier. Right from the beginning of your judging career, keep track of every dog judged in every breed. Don't do as I

do as I did. When first asked for my CV, I said, "Huh?" And then I began compiling and guesstimating entries for the first couple years I judged. I now keep a running total of each year, with 3-year and 10-year totals. I've included a sample at the end of this chapter.

Some foreign host clubs may pay full expenses while the remainder will generally offer partial payment of airfare, lodging, and meal expenses. Very few pay a fee. Foreign judging assignments are, therefore, rarely money making opportunities. Accepting an offer abroad will depend on whether you can afford to make up the difference, how much you like to travel (flights can be horrendously long), and how much you want to see a new country.

Taking on a foreign judging assignment is a wonderful opportunity to see the world without joining the military. Always be sure to ask for the name and address of the hotel you will be staying in advance. Although many people speak English, it's helpful if you know at least a few words in their native language, i.e., thank you and bathroom!

You will find that most foreign clubs/organizations are relaxed in procedure, scheduling, and well, frankly everything. Others, however, are precise and regimented. Many countries ask for a critique of each dog. Some are written, following the show; others are oral and given spontaneously in the ring. Be prepared with a thorough knowledge of the Standards. These people sincerely want to know your evaluation of their dog. If it is to be written, remember to take notes or use a tape recorder while judging.

Naturally, you must judge the dogs according to the Breed Standard of that country. Usually, you will be sent these in advance. If you do not receive them in a timely manner, ask your contact if they are available online. Groups are different in other countries from AKC shows. Many countries are members of the Fédération Cynologique Internationale (FCI). In some countries, you might have to judge breeds you have never seen before. This is a challenge, but if you have an eye for dogs, good examples of the breed always seem to stand out. It's sorting out mediocrity that is difficult. Placements might also be different from those you're used to. You may be required to award Challenge Certificates (CCs, three of which are needed for a Championship) or Reserve Best In Show for example.

The club will assign you a steward who speaks English or supply an interpreter. Most stewards are well trained and will keep you on track, reminding you of placements. In some countries, they check exhibitors into the ring and mark the placements and absentees, leaving you only the necessity of judging. This is a good thing as you may be required to judge well over 200 dogs.

Traveling Overseas
Several months ahead, apply for a passport if you do not already have one. Check to see whether you need a Visa which is often necessary unless you are traveling to western Europe. You can exchange money at an International airport terminal, but most places accept credit cards. They are preferable to use as the credit card company will handle the currency conversion and it will show up on your bill for ease of accounting.

I always schedule my arrival a good 24 hours before the show so I can recover from jet lag. In addition, I like to know (and so do your hosts) that I will arrive prior to the scheduled time of judging. It's best to pack light as airline restrictions differ, and you'll be schlepping luggage through customs. A coat or sweater is a good idea, with a small umbrella. Crushable wash and wear clothes that you can rinse in a sink may work well for you. Depending on the weather and if the show site is indoors or outdoors, bring appropriate layerable outer garments. Pack a foldable bag in your suitcase, so you can bring some goodies home from your travels.

If you're a fussy eater, bring a few snacks such as trail mix, granola bars, crackers, or peanut butter. You don't always have time to eat (or even buy something) in an airport, and it fills the void if you're allergic to fish and that is the only thing on the menu.

Some domestic cell phones will not work overseas. Currently, it is best to obtain a quad band phone, such as that from AT&T or T-Mobile. A Subscriber Identity Module (SIM) card is used for foreign travel. Another suggestion is to set up an account with Accuglobe (www.accuglobe.com). They will give you access codes that enable you to use your phone in other countries. As of this writing, Verizon Wireless will loan customers a global satellite phone.

I like to stay a day or more following the show, if possible, to see the country. After all, what's the sense of an 18+ hour flight being cramped in an airplane seat if you're going to miss seeing the Great Wall of China?

Curriculum Vitae Example

Keep a curriculum vitae of breed numbers. Many foreign kennel clubs want to know your experience in judging the breeds you are invited to preside over in their country. It's easiest to collate these if the CV is divided into one year, three year, and ten year totals. Here is what I use.

2007

Group 1—Sporting	AZ	OR	IL	CA	NC	UK	MO
Pointer				8			5
G. Shorthaired Pointer				7			11
G. Wirehaired Pointer	2						1
Ret. (Ches. Bay)							
Retriever (Golden)				20			14
Retriever (Labrador)				24			16
Setter (English)				19	6		
Setter (Gordon)					1		
Setter (Irish)				14	9		2
Spaniel (Clumber)							
Spaniel (Cocker)							
Spaniel (E. Springer)							
Vizsla (Smooth)							
Weimaraner							

Group 3—Working							
Akita	7						1
Alaskan Malamute	2		8				
Anatolian Shepherd	3			6			
Bernese Mountain Dog	9	31	5				3

Chapter 5

CONVERSATIONS WE WOULD LIKE TO HAVE

Exhibitors and judges alike enjoy what we do, or we wouldn't do it. At least most of us wouldn't. But if we had a magic lantern and a genie to grant our wishes, we'd tip things a bit more in our favor to make the dog show experience even more pleasurable.

Both judges and exhibitors have a right to expect certain things from each other. A judge needs to be fair, honest, patient, and friendly to build the right kind of reputation. Exhibitors need to be courteous, show good sportsmanship, and an understanding of how difficult a task the judge often has. But since dog show judging is at least part art rather than science only, there will be honest differences of opinion.

I am sure that every judge and every exhibitor has muttered things under their breath or at least thought certain things while in the ring. Just imagine if they were able to tell each other exactly what they think and want! What would those snippets of conversations sound like? Both sides often would love to be able to express themselves verbally, especially when they don't see eye-to-eye. Let's listen in on some conversations you might hear in the ring if you were a mind reader.

What a Judge Might Want to Tell an Exhibitor

- Exercise your dog before entering the ring!

- Don't over-groom. Don't use foreign substances on your dog. And while you are at it, remove the sleep crud from your dog's eyes!

- If you want to know my procedures, come and watch a class or two ahead of yours.

- Listen to the steward. Follow my instructions. "Half way down and back," does not mean the full length of the ring.

- Be ringside and ready for your class, Winners, and Reserve. Have another handler ready to take in the "spare" dog(s). Don't block entrances or aisles waiting to enter the ring.

- Don't block my way as I approach to examine your dog.

- Learn how to show your dog's bite/teeth.

- Thank you for being willing to show your dog before me even though you are the only one entered. I am a provisional and need the entry!

- Have your dog trained to handle the in-the-ring experience.

- No cell phones in the ring!

- Don't even think about trying to intimidate me!

- Dress appropriately (and modestly—no peekaboo anything)!

- Stop complaining. It's not always "politics." Realize there may be other good dogs in the ring.
- Clean teeth make a good impression. Dirty teeth, the opposite.

- If you're going to enter in Bred-by-Exhibitor, bring me your best dog, not a point builder.
- If you have another entry in the next class, let me know and have your dogs all ready at ringside and have armbands on in proper order.
- Show only sound dogs.
- Adjust where you set up your dog according to the size of the class.
- Know how to best set up your dog. Please do not lift the dog by the loin, causing the back to roach.
- Don't string up the dog when gaiting.
- Don't grandstand (especially in Juniors)!
- Do your grooming prior to entering the ring. Heavily coated dogs need to be groomed everywhere. Yes, around the testicles too.

- Bait is not supposed to be a meal. Don't feed the dog just before I examine his teeth—and if you toss your bait, pick it up. There is no need to brush constantly. Every hair does not have to be in place.

- No dental braces, tooth caps, or dyed hair on the dogs…these are OK only on humans.

- Don't use excuses if your dog behaves poorly. I don't want to hear, "It's your hat, your glasses, your height, you're wearing pink," or whatever. Just say you are sorry and correct the dog.

- Please set your dog up with his profile toward me for examination. I often have to take more than 10,000 steps a day while judging—I know, sometimes I wear a pedometer. Three more steps to see each dog in profile adds up!

- On the down and back, run right toward me, not three feet one side or the other. I've seen the profile already, so please come straight back.

- Don't run up on each other! It's not a race—slow down.

- Wait for your ribbon in front of the correct placement and say thank you, even if you're disappointed. Be a good sport. Tomorrow is another day, another show, another judge.

- Don't tell me about all the wins your dog has had. As one judge notoriously said, "I can't be responsible for others' mistakes!"

- If you applaud for one dog, clap for all.

- I don't mind if you disagree with me as long as you do so politely.

- Don't ask why I didn't like the dog—ask why the other dog won or what you can do to improve.

- After two or three tries for a nice stance when having a picture taken, try your dog on a sit. Repeated attempts use up my lunch period or potty break!

- If you have a Toy breed showing in a large ring, you don't have to use the whole ring! I can hardly see that far!

- Try to stay and watch your entire breed, or better yet, the entire show and learn something new.

- Have someone videotape you at training class so that you can avoid mistakes and show your dog at the right speed. It's impossible to reward a dog who is lying on his back or who looks more like a horse thundering to the finish line.

- Watch me and pay attention to the action in the ring, rather than chatting—time enough for that later when you show off your ribbons.

- Have fun with your dog!

What an Exhibitor Might Want to Tell a Judge

As I mentioned at the beginning of the book, it is important that a judge never stop learning. In business, they say listen (and learn from) your customers. Exhibitors are our customers and it is the foolish judge who does not realize this. While you may not always want to hear what they say, here are some of the things exhibitors might wish they could tell you while in the ring!

- Talk loud enough that we can hear you and use words, not hand signals.

- Don't chat with someone at ringside when you're supposed to be judging, especially given how hard I have worked to get this far.

- Don't approach my dog from behind, and make sure you know which breeds to approach from the side rather than head on.

- Remember some breeds are not waggy, but reserved.

- Don't expect all breeds to react to strange noises or bait.

- Understand anatomy and movement—please!

- Judge only the breeds you are truly interested in. And don't rush through a breed that isn't one of your favorites!

- Wait for me to set up my dog, give me a chance to show you my dog at his best.

- My dog might break his stance if you talk to him. If that happens, let me set up the dog again—and try to keep quiet.

- If you have a class run around the ring first, show the same courtesy to a single entry.

- Actually examine my dog—don't simply make a swipe down the topline.

- Look at all sides of my dog.

- Look at the Winners in all the classes, not just Open.

- Watch the dogs, not the handlers, no matter how good looking! Don't judge a dog by its ads or ranking, but by the Standard.

- Look for the best dog, not just for flashy color or performance.

- Don't overlook a dog that's out of coat.

- Don't put up over-grooming or trimming that is incorrect according to the Standard or the use of improper products in the coat.

- If in doubt, measure or weigh.

- Look for good conditioning.

- Don't allow my fellow exhibitors to run up on dogs ahead of them.

- Don't play the "Does WB or WD have the most points?" game with me. Just put up the best dog.

- Remember the influence your choice may have on my future breeding programs.

- Don't push my puppy beyond his limits. If he is misbehaving, I am OK with you excusing him or putting him at the end. One bad day could ruin a puppy's career.

- Don't use my dog to balance yourself or to bear your weight.

- Just because you count teeth on one breed, it's not necessary to do this in all breeds unless required in the Standard.

- Don't do favors for anyone. Somebody—maybe you—always comes out a loser.

- If the dog is within the correct size, don't discount it just because it's the smallest or the largest.

- If dividing the class into groups, don't forget to bring back the other (or first) group!

- Don't gossip about dogs—you never know who might overhear you!

- Use wet wipes to remove drool from your hands before going on to my dog. Same thing after going over a bitch in season.

- Better to withhold ribbons if the dog is unworthy or of poor breed type than to reward mediocrity.

- Remember two things when making placements: Could the dog function? Would you take the dog home for a breeding program?

- If the color is correct under the Standard, don't be color prejudiced.

- Markings, if correct, should not sway your judgment.

- If in doubt about eye color, check it out of direct light.

- Don't try to determine whether my dog has good hips, patellas, hearing, or other health issues. You're a judge, not a veterinarian. And even if you are a vet, the ring isn't the place!

- Ask the steward for dogs' ages in Bred-by-Exhibitor. Many puppies are shown in this class.
- If we have a large, moving breed in a small ring, let us move around enough to show the best gait.
- Require a loose lead and enforce it.
- Don't tolerate rude behavior.
- If two (or three) choices are very close, move them together or go over them again, showing us handlers that our dogs are under serious consideration.
- Be patient with and help the newbies! We want them to come back to help grow our sport.
- If you cannot handle the physical stress of a show, stay home. Think about retirement!

A once-upon-a-time saying was "If wishes were horses, then beggars would ride." It's unlikely everyone in dogdom will remember all of these wishes, but if we all try to grant some of them, at least we won't be last in the race!

Chapter 6

WAR STORIES
THE BEST AND THE
WORST OF TIMES

Everyone who's shown or judged a few years has tales of horror and humor to tell. These can be the best of times or the worst of times. Whether you are showing or judging, you'd better pack your sense of humor every time you head to a show.

Getting There is Half the Fun
Arctic blasts, blizzards, monsoons, floods. Dog show people don't let the weather stop them. At one show, it rained so hard that a nearby dam actually burst and threatened to flood the show grounds. Not one to give up, an exhibitor asked if the judge couldn't just finish Open and Winners before fleeing to higher ground! At another show, it was so cold that one devoted owner with two puppies (who were happily cuddled together wrapped in towels and blankets) had to chip away half an inch of ice inside the car built up from the pups' breath! At that same show, a judge tells me he had to clean up sticky brown "snow" caused by a soft drink can that had exploded. Who knows, sticky brown snow caused by something else at a dog show could be even worse, I guess!

* * * * *

Before the era of the GPS, if you were on your way to a show but unsure of its location, following a car with dog crates and cute doggie bumper stickers always seemed to be a good idea...until the driver turned into some vet clinic or a private driveway. It was always pretty maddening to find a whole "pack" of stranded dog people standing around looking at each other and fumbling for a map. My other personal favorite is forgetting there's a time zone change along the route—oops! These are the times we hit the accelerator, change quickly in the car, and then eventually dash into the ring. This is why I've invested in a GPS and radar detector.

* * * * *

An exhibitor took a "spoiled, demanding" Chinese Crested puppy on a road trip in order to socialize the dog at the National. As she stopped for a much-needed break, the pup vocalized her objection at being left in the car by screaming her protest to the world. The owner returned to find the car surrounded by a gang of Hells Angels. Gulping, she approached the group who wanted to know what "this little, skinny bald dog, with giant hair, sitting on a big fluffy pink dog bed screaming like a car alarm" was. Answering that led to another question, and another. She wound up holding a seminar, along with handouts, in the middle of a truck stop parking lot. Who knows how many Angels now own a Crested?

Groaning Inwardly

We all dread the extreme weather days. The only time I felt sorry for a friend winning was at a show grounds that ended up with about six inches of standing water in and around the rings. She bathed and groomed her Beardie three times, once each before Breed, Group, and Best In Show. Then she had to bathe him again to bring him into the house.

* * * * *

On a day when thunder crashed, lightning slashed the skies and it rained, yes, Persians and Dobermans, I was scheduled in three different rings. As the exhibitors looked at me pleadingly and the dogs shivered, I called a halt in my ring. We huddled under the tent, but in retrospect it was not a good idea. A creek that had been non-existent just an hour before ran through one ring. Another ring was moved halfway onto asphalt, while the other half remained in mud. Since I was running about 45 minutes late, I skipped lunch and my steward brought me some fruit for me to munch on between classes. Lesson: Take care of your people, and they'll take care of you.

* * * * *

Dogs have great scenting ability! Don't drown yourself in perfume. At one show several dogs continued to back away from a judge who'd bathed in aftershave.

* * * * *

A handler bent down to adjust her dog and clunked heads with the judge. As the judge waited to clear his head, the handler began choking on a piece of hot dog that had shot into her airway after the collision. She came in last, but luckily for her she coughed up the hot dog and survived.

* * * * *

Showing and judging Komondors can be a challenge. Dogs with short cords compete against mature dogs with glorious long cords. And then there are the long cords which tend to hide a lot of things, including the leash. At one show, the handler dropped her white leash when setting up the dog and couldn't find it again when the judge asked if she was ready to go around. Looking up she blurted, "No," which irritated the judge. Needless to say her dog didn't win. "Next time," she said, "I'll just pick up a cord and use it as a leash."

Faux Paws

We all make "faux paws" now and then, particularly when doing something new. A novice was judging Best In Match for the first time. Concentrating on her decision, she examined the dogs, then sent them around and awarded first through fourth (oops!). The exhibitors chuckled and said, "That's ok; now we know what you think about our dogs!"

* * * * *

The English have the best sense of humor! At lunch a steward asked a visiting British judge who was new to the breed, "How did it go?" The judge answered, "Well dear, to be perfectly honest, I completely lost the plot after puppy dog and judged the owners' shoes instead from junior class onward." She added, "And I must have done a reasonable job as the breed president has just told me it was the finest piece of judging he's seen in twenty years and asked me to judge their Specialty!"

* * * * *

Ladies have to be careful about wearing large or noisy jewelry or something that clunks the dog in the head as we bend over for the examination. A Poodle judge—and an exhibitor—were embarrassed when the judge's ring became caught in the topknot of the dog and pulled the switch off. Another had to extract her ring when it became entangled in an Old English Sheepdog's carefully coiffed "do." Spectators at both rings could be heard guffawing.

* * * * *

A first-time English judge dismissed all the top winners in Wheatens. When queried later as to why he didn't like the top dog, the judge said, "I plucked this ear of wheat, and I have compared all the dogs to this colour as described in the Standard, and let me tell you, sir, that your dog's colour does not compare to the colour of this wheat, and I am the judge." The exhibitor replied, "Well, you may be the judge, but I'm a farmer and that's not wheat, that's barley."

The Judge's View
One of the best known anecdotes happened in the ring of Dorothy Nickels, a well-known judge. An exhibitor whispered to her that the dog only needed a point to finish its Championship. Miss Dorothy didn't blink an eye. She asked the other exhibitors how many points each of their dogs needed, then said, "Now that we know where everybody stands, let's get back to judging dogs." Miss Dorothy always remembered to pack her humor.

* * * * *

Many Standards discourage or fault trimming. After one National, a judge who'd despaired about finding too many dogs who'd visited a canine barber said tongue-in-cheek, "If you're going to trim, do both sides!"

* * * * *

The habit of "double handling" German Shepherds puzzles and sometimes annoys everyone except German Shepherd exhibitors. This practice started in Germany and continues here because people are under the impression that judges must see the ears up at all times, with the dog alerting. Owners stand (or run) outside the ring, sometimes clanging a bell, holding a much loved dog toy, calling names or doing whatever it takes to alert the dog's attention. Once I've seen the ears up, I don't need to again, so being a former Shepherd exhibitor, I find the best results come from handling this practice with humor. "Sit, stay!" directed at the "outside" handler usually works for me. Another breeder judge suggested, "If you want to learn to do this right (i.e., subtly), see me after the show. I'll give you lessons."

* * * * *

Judges enjoy wearing holiday clothing, whether ties, jewelry, or sweaters. I had a sweater decked out with reindeer and a tree, and snowball pompons covering the buttons. As I bent over a Doberman puppy, he gently reached up and snipped off one of the pompons, standing there holding the piece of fluff between his teeth. His owner was embarrassed, the dog was nonplussed as though he were thinking "I thought this was a marshmallow. Now what do I do?" And I was laughing so hard I could barely continue judging.

* * * * *

Judges hear a plethora of excuses for a dog's poor behavior: "This is her first show/weekend/show with me/season" or "This is only his third time out." Finally after I'd heard several excuses, one adult behaved particularly poorly. I mumbled to the steward, "And this is only his seventeenth time out."

* * * * *

An esteemed judge had a young child in his ring. During the examination of the child's dog, the judge discovered the dog had only one testicle. While he deliberated how to tell the child, he decided to ask if his parents were ringside, then asked if he could speak to them. The boy asked, "Did my dog take up his ball?" Taken by surprise, the judge answered affirmatively. The child picked up the dog, cheerily said, "He does that all the time," and left the ring.

Another time, same scenario, different handler and judge. He said quietly, "Ma'am, did you realize your dog has only one testicle?" Her loud response was: "I know, but ain't it a beaut?"

* * * * *

We can't seem to stay away from dog shows even when not on the panel, so one judge volunteered to steward for another judge. First a dog defecated on a side mat, followed by another going on the diagonal. The steward called for clean-up and finally left the ring to search for a scooper, leaving the judge observing the results of a good diet. Two ladies from a local nursing home, on a day trip, said to one another, "They judge that too?" Our ever helpful steward joked, "Yes, it cannot be removed until evaluated by the judge and if, up to standard, it will be helpful to the dog." The two ladies spread the word to the other folks present. The steward later confessed her tall tale to all of them.

Call Me Ishmael

One time after judging a specialty in Mexico City, I discovered, after checking my boarding pass, I was no longer who I thought I was. I was now Ishmael Cortez. Hmmmmm, did no one notice this as I passed through security, comparing my passport to my pass? As my fellow judges appeared and stood in the boarding line, I thought, "I'd better do something or I'll be living as Ishmael in Mexico for the rest of my life." I spoke with the gate agent, who casually said, "I'll take care of this. Just have a seat." Announcements were soon made for Ishmael, who showed up to claim his boarding pass, but did not have mine. The gate agent looked at me and said "Your papers will be coming soon." Everyone boarded the plane...still no boarding pass. Finally, the agent shrugged and said, "Oh, well, get on. We know who you are." Not one to argue about a happy ending, I scurried on the plane. I'm still wondering who's now living in the USA under my name.

* * * * *

While judging in India, we took a side trip to a tiger sanctuary in Ranthamb-hore. Unfortunately, the driver hired for us did not speak English and did not know the way. At each (unmarked) fork in the road, he would turn and ask us directions in Hindi. We'd shrug and he'd choose a road, driving until he saw a rock with the name of the next town painted on it or stopping a pedestrian to ask. The car kept shimmying to a stop (possibly due to driving through creek beds, huge potholes, and over rocks), and the driver would disembark, jiggle something and then continue on. The trip was supposed to take six hours. It took nine, but seemed longer. When we were in the countryside, the only light was from bonfires in the villages. At one point, when it was as dark as the inside of a sacred cow's stomach, our driver screamed, "Billy! Billy, Billy, Billy!" He leaped out of the car and disappeared. As we looked at each other, another man came up to the car and jerked open the door and got in. Was this "Billy"? At this point, I thought our kids would be reading about an American couple lost forever in India. Then our driver returned and he and the other man talked back and forth to each other in an animated way. Then our driver threw something across the road, jiggled under the hood, and took we off down the road again.

A couple days later, when my nerves were settled, I asked our host at the tiger sanctuary what this could possibly have meant. After some consultation, he said, "Ahhhhhhhhhhhhh, black cat cross road. Driver throw stick or rock across road to break curse." In my mind, the tigers were less frightening than the trip to get there!

As a footnote to this story, the way back to the airport took only six hours, but it seemed longer because our new driver played Indian rock music all the way back and drove on sidewalks to get us to our destination.

* * * * *

After landing in Indonesia many years ago, a judge was picked up by a bejew-eled fellow who led her to his limo. On the way, the host asked, "So how do you feel about Pomeranians with bad bites?" She responded, "I couldn't place such a dog." He was silent for a moment, then said, "Sooooooooooooooo how do you feel about Boxers?" As they reached the car, she noticed another judge waiting who immediately grasped her arm and said, "Thank God you're here. He's been driving me around buying me gifts I don't want and showing me pictures of his Boxer." Our ethical judge said, "We'll just judge the dogs as we see fit." The next day, the judge saw an impressive Boxer walk in her Best In Show ring, one that stood out and was the easy winner. Yes, it did turn out to be the same Boxer. No pictures needed.

* * * * *

While judging in Colombia, I was warned not to touch the Fila Brazilieros, a breed new to me. This breed was developed to be a tough guard dog, so I decided to err on the side of caution and listen to the warning. I walked to the front of the dogs and from a safe distance, asked each handler to show me the bite. They would then stretch the skin on the head for me to see the pliability of the skin. I walked to the side, where they stretched the skin on the neck and back. As I walked to the rear of the dogs, they showed me the dog's testicles by bouncing them, boing, boing, boing. Why three boings, I don't know, and I didn't ask.

* * * * *

My very long day of travel began when the airport reservations clerk told me, "Cargo is broken." "Excuse me?" I replied. She went on, "You have the choice of being separated from your suitcase or taking a later flight." Well, taking a later flight was not an option. A club member was driving two hours to pick me up. So I hurriedly switched things between my carry-on and my soon-to-be-separated suitcase and went on, hoping my larger bag would arrive later and be delivered.

Once we were settled in the plane, the flight attendant shuffled some unhappy people from the first three rows to the rear to better balance the weight. As we heard some strange noises underneath us, we were told that steel bars were being loaded to make up for the lack of baggage weight. As we took off, the steel bars went THUNK, THUNK, sliding to the rear of cargo. And, later, when we nosed down to land, the familiar THUNK, THUNK banged toward the front of the plane, as we all prayed they wouldn't crash through the plane and land on some poor unsuspecting person. Safe on land, as we waited for another judge to arrive, I checked baggage, and there it was. My suitcase had arrived before I did.

We arrived at the town where the show was being held, late and starving. The room clerk said, "Sorry, we have no reservation for you, and we're full." By this time, I was sporting a deer-in-the-headlights expression, and another judge took pity on me and offered me the other bed in her room. The restaurant was totally booked too. By this time, the floor, an extra pillow, and a Twinkie sounded good.

* * * * *

Don't believe it when the hotel tells you your flight crew is leaving at a certain time on the shuttle, so you will have plenty of time. Naively, I waited and waited for the pilot who arrived ten minutes late, making me two minutes late to put my bags in cargo. The next flight would mean a missed connection, so I gritted my teeth, madly tossing away about $100 worth of liquids—perfume, makeup, meds—in order to dash through security. The really annoying part was arriving home to find four things I'd missed throwing away, but security didn't catch.

* * * * *

Be flexible. After an exhausting trip home from overseas, my plane landed too late to make the final connection. I grabbed 4 hours sleep in a motel and hurried to the airport the next morning. We took off, and I looked forward to being in my own bed that night. As we neared my home airport, a haze rolled in, and we circled for over an hour. By now low on fuel, we then headed for another airport 250 miles away from my home sweet home. After an hour's wait, we discovered the next flight would take us back to the airport we had started from that morning. So some of us rented a car and drove the five hours home while others decided to take the flight. That night I slept in my own bed. Who knows where the others were? I didn't care.

* * * * *

Many of us forget to remove our judge's badge before dining out or heading back home. After a gentleman called me "Your Honor" at an airport, I wondered what advantages this could bring me.

* * * * *

Judges have none of the usual job benefits, i.e., pensions or health insurance. Our vacations usually consist of a couple extra days after a show in an area touring or visiting friends. Holidays are often spent judging. This is not a complaint, but, because of this, many judges have other jobs. One of our ranks works for an airline and related a story about a trip to Russia during the Cold War. They were put up at a hotel where a crew member stubbed his toe on an object hidden under the carpet. Pulling back the carpet, he discovered a black box. "The dirty !@#$%," he thought. "They're bugging us!" He said, "I'll fix them," and dug out his tool box. Working diligently, he managed to dislodge the box which had been bolted to the floor. Just underneath him, the dining room chandelier fell down.

Less Than Perfect Moments

After a weekend of judging in 105 degree heat at a fairgrounds, a few of us faced red-eye flights. Feeling filthy and dripping wet, I had a brainstorm and asked if there were showers on the grounds and was told there were. The Show Chair found us soap, and I relished feeling the dirt and sweat wash off me. Unfortunately, the soap fell out of my slick hands and headed under the shower grate. I was determined to get the elusive bar and knelt down to feel under the grate, pulling it out covered with cobwebs, praying no one would walk into the room as there were no shower curtains. Feeling much better following the shower, I realized I had no towel, so used my sweaty, sodden dress to dry off with and donned fresh clothes ready to face the night-long flight. This is why we take our vitamins.

* * * * *

We experienced travelers (most judges are) learn to lock and chain our doors the second we walk into our hotel room. Many of us have either walked into a room already occupied by someone else or had someone walk into our room, through a check-in glitch. This can be embarrassing, depending on the stage of dress or undress of the occupant. On one trip, I had a zipper stuck on my slacks and couldn't get out of them. After I worked on it for some time, followed by my husband being equally unsuccessful, I felt the urgency of the situation and said, "Just rip it." As he proceeded to rip it, the maid walked in, gasped…and quickly walked out.

* * * * *

Several years ago on the way to Westminster, a friend and I were snowed in at St. Louis. We managed to obtain what must have been the last room in the city. After a taxi similar to that in the movie "Planes, Trains and Automobiles" dropped us off, we timidly checked in at the desk, where a sign proudly proclaimed: *Those using the room less than 15 minutes will be charged the full rate.* We put a chair under the door knob and slept in our clothes. Desperation makes strange stays.

Things That Could Never Happen Today!

Years ago, when a group of judges were engaging in one of our favorite pastimes, i.e., complaining about the length and difficulty of advancing in the judging ranks, an all-breed judge told us about an experience she had. At that time, the acquisition of certain "key breeds" granted a judge Group status. The Powers That Be decided which breeds a judge would be allowed. After waiting some time to be approved for a key breed, she was told to go to a show and watch a breeder judge. She then had to critique the judge's choices and to draw a picture of the breed. Well, she was admittedly a stick figure kind of artist, and she didn't like any of the choices the breeder judge made. After a two-day interview, she was approved! Moral: Count your blessings—drawing skills and two day interviews are a thing of the past!

* * * * *

Many years ago, a judge told an exhibitor he was showing the dog wrong, took the lead out of his hand, ran the dog down and back, and then put the dog Winners!

* * * * *

An exhibitor was told by the same judge that he did not love his dog and instructed him to sit on the floor in the middle of the ring with his arms around the dog. She judged the entire class, excluding the one in the center, then pointed him as Winners!

* * * * *

A man who became a much admired judge was approved for one breed, Collies. He was asked to judge a match and became flummoxed when asked to judge Bulldogs. He said he finally figured he'd put up the one that looked least like a Collie.

* * * * *

One judge, who is also a neurosurgeon, said it took him longer to become a judge than a doctor. Maybe it is because the AKC has over 150 breeds, while humans have only one brain.

Great Quotes That Have Served Me Well

- "I'd like to buy this dog for what I think it is worth and sell him for what you think he's worth."
- "Make your mistakes quickly."
- "The dogs don't get any better the longer you look at them." (And sometimes they become worse!)
- "Be true to yourself. You're the one who looks in the mirror."
- "Judging is more of an art than a science."

A Parting Thought

Every once in a while, we find a dog that makes our heart sing. This is why we put up with disappointments, erratic airplane schedules, and sorting through dogs of less than sterling quality. When we find a puppy we can carry through to Best of Breed, a newcomer with an outstanding dog, or "discover" a new star, what fun it is to be a judge!

INDEX

ABOUT THE AUTHOR

Chris Walkowicz began showing and breeding German Shepherds in 1965, adding Bearded Collies in 1977. More than 50 Walkoway Beardies and Shepherds finished their Championships and Register of Merits, and nearly 60 boast performance titles. Chris began judging in 1995 and has judged in the US and all over the world. She is approved to judge all the Herding, Working, and Sporting breeds and groups, Best In Show, Miscellaneous and Juniors.

Chris is an award-winning author of many books and articles on dog-related subjects, including *Successful Dog Breeding* and *The Atlas of Dog Breeds of the World*. Her awards include Dog Writer Association of America (DWAA) Best Book, Book of the Month Club selection, National League of American Pen Women Best Non-fiction book and a top reference book choice from the National Library Association. She has served as an officer and on the board of the Bearded Collie Club of America, as well as several other dog clubs. Chris lives in Sherrand, Illinois.

Ed and Chris in Australia.

From Dogwise Publishing, www.dogwise.com, 1-800-776-2665

BEHAVIOR & TRAINING

ABC's of Behavior Shaping. Proactive Behavior Mgmt, DVD set. Ted Turner

Aggression In Dogs. Practical Mgmt, Prevention, & Behaviour Modification. Brenda Aloff

Am I Safe? DVD. Sarah Kalnajs

Barking. The Sound of a Language. Turid Rugaas

Behavior Problems in Dogs, 3rd ed. William Campbell

Brenda Aloff's Fundamentals: Foundation Training for Every Dog, DVD. Brenda Aloff

Bringing Light to Shadow. A Dog Trainer's Diary. Pam Dennison

Canine Body Language. A Photographic Guide to the Native Language of Dogs. Brenda Aloff

Clicked Retriever. Lana Mitchell

Dog Behavior Problems. The Counselor's Handbook. William Campbell

Dog Friendly Gardens, Garden Friendly Dogs. Cheryl Smith

Dog Language, An Encyclopedia of Canine Behavior. Roger Abrantes

Dogs are from Neptune, 2nd ed.. Jean Donaldson

Evolution of Canine Social Behavior, 2nd ed. Roger Abrantes

From Hoofbeats to Dogsteps. A Life of Listening to and Learning from Animals. Rachel Page Elliott

Get Connected With Your Dog, book with DVD. Brenda Aloff

Give Them a Scalpel and They Will Dissect a Kiss, DVD. Ian Dunbar

Guide to Professional Dog Walking And Home Boarding. Dianne Eibner

Language of Dogs, DVD. Sarah Kalnajs

Mastering Variable Surface Tracking, Component Tracking (2 bk set). Ed Presnall

My Dog Pulls. What Do I Do? Turid Rugaas

New Knowledge of Dog Behavior (reprint). Clarence Pfaffenberger

Oh Behave! Dogs from Pavlov to Premack to Pinker. Jean Donaldson

On Talking Terms with Dogs. Calming Signals, 2nd edition. Turid Rugaas

On Talking Terms with Dogs. What Your Dog Tells You, DVD. Turid Rugaas

Play With Your Dog. Pat Miller

Positive Perspectives. Love Your Dog, Train Your Dog. Pat Miller

Positive Perspectives 2. Know Your Dog, Train Your Dog. Pat Miller

Predation and Family Dogs, DVD. Jean Donaldson

Really Reliable Recall. Train Your Dog to Come When Called, DVD. Leslie Nelson

Right on Target. Taking Dog Training to a New Level. Mandy Book & Cheryl Smith

Stress in Dogs. Martina Scholz & Clarissa von Reinhardt

Tales of Two Species. Essays on Loving and Living With Dogs. Patricia McConnell

The Dog Trainer's Resource. The APDT Chronicle of the Dog Collection. Mychelle Blake (*ed*)

The Dog Trainer's Resource 2. The APDT Chronicle of the Dog Collection. Mychelle Blake (*ed*)

The Thinking Dog. Crossover to Clicker Training. Gail Fisher

Therapy Dogs. Training Your Dog To Reach Others. Kathy Diamond Davis

Training Dogs. A Manual (reprint). Konrad Most

Training the Disaster Search Dog. Shirley Hammond

Try Tracking. The Puppy Tracking Primer. Carolyn Krause

Visiting the Dog Park, Having Fun, and Staying Safe. Cheryl S. Smith

When Pigs Fly. Train Your Impossible Dog. Jane Killion

Winning Team. A Guidebook for Junior Showmanship. Gail Haynes

Working Dogs (reprint). Elliot Humphrey & Lucien Warner

HEALTH & ANATOMY, SHOWING

An Eye for a Dog. Illustrated Guide to Judging Purebred Dogs. Robert Cole

Annie On Dogs! Ann Rogers Clark

Another Piece of the Puzzle. Pat Hastings

Canine Cineradiography DVD. Rachel Page Elliott

Canine Massage. A Complete Reference Manual. Jean-Pierre Hourdebaigt

Canine Terminology (reprint). Harold Spira

Breeders Professional Secrets. Ethical Breeding Practices. Sylvia Smart

Dog In Action (reprint). Macdowell Lyon

Dogsteps DVD. Rachel Page Elliott

The Healthy Way to Stretch Your Dog. A Physical Theraphy Approach. Sasha Foster and Ashley Foster

The History and Management of the Mastiff. Elizabeth Baxter & Pat Hoffman

Performance Dog Nutrition. Optimize Performance With Nutrition. Jocelynn Jacobs

Positive Training for Show Dogs. Building a Relationship for Success Vicki Ronchette

Puppy Intensive Care. A Breeder's Guide To Care Of Newborn Puppies. Myra Savant Harris

Raw Dog Food. Make It Easy for You and Your Dog. Carina MacDonald

Raw Meaty Bones. Tom Lonsdale

Shock to the System. The Facts About Animal Vaccination... Catherine O'Driscoll

Tricks of the Trade. From Best of Intentions to Best in Show, Rev. Ed. Pat Hastings

Work Wonders. Feed Your Dog Raw Meaty Bones. Tom Lonsdale

Whelping Healthy Puppies, DVD. Sylvia Smart

Dogwise.com is your complete source for dog books on the web!

2,000+ titles, fast shipping, and excellent customer service.